T0078007

HARNESS

--- THE ---

POWER

--- OF ---

PURPOSE

HOW TO MONETIZE YOUR PERSONAL
AND BUSINESS JOURNEY

A COLLABORATIVE WORK
WITH
MICHAEL BART MATHEWS

Order this book online at www.trafford.com
or email orders@trafford.com

Most Trafford titles are also available at major online book retailers.

Editor-In-Chief: Natalie M. Bonomo of Wisconsin
Contributor: Robbie S. Mathews

Print information available on the last page.

ISBN: 978-1-6987-0265-0 (sc)
ISBN: 978-1-6987-0266-7 (hc)
ISBN: 978-1-6987-0267-4 (e)

Library of Congress Control Number: 2020914605

Because of the dynamic nature of the Internet, any web addresses or links contained in
this book may have changed since publication and may no longer be valid. The views
expressed in this work are solely those of the author and do not necessarily reflect the
views of the publisher, and the publisher hereby disclaims any responsibility for them.

Any people depicted in stock imagery provided by Getty Images are models, and such
images are being used for illustrative purposes only.
Certain stock imagery © Getty Images.

Trafford rev. 09/29/2020

 www.trafford.com
North America & international
toll-free: 1 888 232 4444 (USA & Canada)
fax: 812 355 4082

CONTENTS

PART 4 THE NON-PROFIT WORLD
IT'S BETTER TO GIVE THAN TO
RECEIVE (ACTS 20:35 KJV)

FOREWORD

This book brings a select group of subject matter experts together to offer the reader the keys to creating success in one's business and, more importantly, in life. Michael Bart Mathews displays a real gift in his writing, publishing, and authentic communication that shines brightly throughout this entire book. I highly recommend this masterful expression for achieving real success.

There is immense power in becoming an effective communicator. Communication is the real currency of our time. Excellent communications with others and oneself leads to focus, commitment, and positive habits that breed success in every great achievement. This book shares the power of focused thought, the secrets to creating an economic machine, the unlimited resources in collaboration, and finding real purpose by giving back! Great job, Mike, and to all your authors, we thank you for sharing your gifts.

—Dr. James Dentley
Founder of Inspired2Speak

INTRODUCTION

If anyone's gonna write about me, I reckon it be me, myself.
—Langston Hughes

We gazed out into the world, starting with our communities and saw that a great multitude of people was mentally, physically, and financially scorched with failure, pain, suffering, grief, sorrow, and hopelessness. We looked at the cause and discovered that those same people were moving around day-in-and-day-out like walking zombies who had flatlined on the operating table, having no signs of brain waves or function, or a heartbeat toward success. No, they were not gracefully living; they were busy mentally, physically, spiritually, and financially dying.

During this publication, the coronavirus has exceeded over 14,774,887 confirmed cases worldwide. This pandemic is causing an incredible amount of pain, suffering, and 611,599 untimely deaths, as reported by global news. Over forty-million Americans filed for unemployment assistance. There are an estimated 174 million unemployed people worldwide at the time of this publication. The homeless are experiencing a never-before kind of helplessness. To help ease the financial burden, the US government issued $1,200 stimulus checks for adults and $500 for children to help stimulate the economy. My fellow American's, think back. How long did that government check last? Because of COVID-19, a higher level of uncertainty and fear of health and financial devastation is now deeply rooted in the thoughts and minds of Americans and our global citizens, elsewhere in the world.

We are your entrepreneurs, your financial professionals, your small business owners, your mom and pop kitchen table startups. We are your nonprofits, stepping up and serving at a higher level. We are all for one and one for all, standing together within the pages of this book.

We understood that the remaining Tribal Leaders from the Greatest Generation (1901-1924) are taking their stories to their graves faster than they can tell them to those younger souls who are willing to listen. Those willing souls who are ready and willing to step up and accept the torch that lights the rites of passage from one generation to the next.

We understood this mindset of fear to be a growing problematic, destructive pattern—a mentality of change that must be reverse-engineered within the thoughts of multiple generations.

We understood that this mental weed of self-defeat deeply rooted itself within the minds and thoughts of millions of people from all walks of life, across all generations. We understood that this type of self-destructive mental hopelessness ran rampant throughout our communities. Like the gardener, we recognized the need to till away the weeds of death from the topsoil. For that mineral-rich topsoil covering the seed of life is what allows the birth and growth of a bountiful harvest—a new generation.

We understood that the mineral-rich human mind does not care if you plant the infectious seeds of thoughts which produced weeds of self-defeat. It also does not care if you plant the transformational seeds of thought which produce business development, personal growth, and success. We understood that the mineral-rich human mind would return to you exactly what you plant inside of your thoughts. In other words, we become what we plant and think about in our thoughts.

This book was written by a select group of successful business leaders and entrepreneurs from across the United States. They will share PURPOSE, meaning the ability for which something is done or created, and they will share POWER, indicating the ability to do something or act in a particular way resulting in achievement and success.

While reading this book, you will smell the enticing aroma of personal and business transformation, while seeing the illuminating light for change. You will feel the warm flames from your burning desire for achieving "that special something." Your mouth will begin to salivate with anticipation for the sweet taste of success. You will hear the bells of giving and service to others ring loud for those souls who need a helping hand.

Albert Einstein – "It is the definition of insanity doing the same things over and over again and expecting different results." The journey of identifying your purpose and harnessing the power of your purpose takes a unique set of master keys. To discover your master keys, you cannot keep doing what you have always done, because you will most certainly keep getting what you have always gotten! Together, those master keys will first unlock and next unleash the power of your purpose for being here on earth. But first, you must find your moment of clarity and discover your power of purpose within.

Each author brings to the table a unique and distinctive set of business acumen full of resources, life experience, education, training, and service that can assist you in discovering your purpose and power within. Using each author's knowledge, experience and understanding of how to solve personal and business issues are important key factors for achievement and success, within the pages of this book.

In many cases PURPOSE reveals itself during or after someone goes through adversity. While going through difficulty, they discover seeds of greatness and begin to outline solutions for change. Their newfound purpose is to help others avoid the same misfortune that they experienced. Life has an abundance of shiny objects that are overflowing with distractions. These distractions often happen more frequently early in life. Many adolescents and young adults mentally are sidetracked from being aware of what purpose means and the power needed to advance the objective.

After reading these next few lines, close your eyes for a moment. Now think back to when you were an adolescent. You did not have a care in the world. You dreamt of being a doctor, a professional athlete, a singer, actor, a firefighter, a police officer, a teacher, a lawyer, an airplane pilot, a businessman/woman, a parent, or a loving spouse.

The authors in this book found their purpose and discovered how to harness the power of achievement in using their diverse backgrounds. Their professional services consist of mastering the art of speaking and becoming an effective communicator.

Discover how to manage through a financial downturn and survive through a famine (COVID–19). Explore why it takes a tribe to raise a financially stable village using affiliate partnerships and membership programs to build wealth by being good stewards of your finances. Review how to focus on building relationships along your S.M.A.R.T. – Authentic journey. Lastly, using the power of the spoken word to communicate your purpose, and the servant leadership purpose-driven non-profit sector of providing a hand-up and not a hand-out for change.

The poor souls who could not make that distinction, and stayed distracted, did not have a clear purpose. The underlying challenge most people face in pursuit of identifying their power of purpose is finding clarity, focus, the ability to take action and execute results. Knowing your intentions is one master key to finding your purpose.

The word purpose is tossed around a lot in today's conversations. As we are developing a more enlightened picture of ourselves, and the needs of our global communities, millions of people are taking a deeper dive into self-actualization and personal empowerment for change. Without knowing your power, when you first begin to focus on your purpose, uncertainty lingers. Your purpose should give clarity in your thinking, and your power should provide you with direction for your action plan. As you mature in life, as you identify your purpose, your power will gain the needed strength to move mountains. Power is about having a positive mindset about how you think, feel and act about your purpose.

Each chapter is full of different pain points, and more importantly, they are overflowing with robust solutions for change and results that you seek. The benefits outweigh the pain. Without adversity and suffering, there is no need for change. Life would be easy. We all have some difficulty and pain in our lives that we want to overcome. Reading this book will help you overcome adversity in several different areas, such as speaking and communicating, personal and business finances, and building wealth using affiliate/membership programs. You will discover how to make sound decisions concerning real estate transactions, build strong, empowering relationships, and how to use spoken word to communicate your message. And the art of the non-profit world seen through the eyes of a servant community leader who helps young women will be highlighted.

While succeeding in realizing our life purpose, our authenticity is imperative. Our spiritual light, energy, and awareness is the most genuine connection to our authentic self. Someone said that we are spiritual beings, having human experiences. What we achieve from our human experience can be attributed to the level of knowing our purpose and harnessing the power of our spirit in a positive, productive, results-driven manner.

Our thoughts are attached to our belief systems which provides us with a (good, bad, right, or wrong) mental roadmap toward our destiny here on earth. Your thoughts could be good, bad, right or wrong, however, consciously or subconsciously, our thoughts turn into the things that we think about.

We invite you to take your rightful seat around the Tribal Wealth United personal and business leadership campfire. We, the authors, will share our thoughts and stories. Some of our stories will be personal, and some will be financial and business leadership related. Others will be relationship-related and service-related. We represent a wide array of experience and knowledge like our ancestors did hundreds of years ago.

As you read each amazing chapter, imagine sitting around the campfire with us. Picture yourself surrounded by the Tribal Leaders (authors) who wrote this book. Together, we are seated under the cloak of darkness with the midnight blue sky as our canopy. Take a deep breath and smell the fresh air as we gaze up into the universe and watch the twinkling of the stars. See the ray of light from the moon shining down upon our campsite. Listen carefully to the natural screeching sounds of the owl coming from the forest. Tune in as Mother Nature sings her songs from the howling winds blowing and whistling throughout the trees.

Smell the smoke from the wood burning in the campfire. Relish the relaxing warm heat from the wavy motion of the flickering flames above the burning wood. Enjoy the snap, crackle, and pop as the sparks fly high above the campfire.

Picture the face of each author and listen to the sounds of their voices while you read one amazing chapter after another. Imagine you are eagerly waiting to see, hear, smell, taste, and feel more from the next author's empowering leadership storytelling abilities as you read on.

Your mission is to find your purpose, harness your spirit power, and go out there and change the world! This book is your gateway for change in that which you seek.

In the words of Harriet Tubman, "Every great dream begins with a dreamer. Always remember, you have within you the strength, the patience, and the passion to reach for the stars, to change the world."

—Michael Bart Mathews

PART 1

Effective Communication For Entrepreneurs And Business Owners

CHAPTER 1

IS YOUR VOICE BEING HEARD?

By Dr. Janice Hooker Fortman

The biggest single problem in communication
is the illusion that it has taken place.
—George Bernard Shaw

Have you ever been in a situation where you said something to someone, and your communication was misunderstood or ignored? In the words of Chris Tucker from the movie *Rush Hour*, you will no longer have to say, "Do you understand the words that are coming out of my mouth?" We often assume that just because we say something and the other person does not understand what we mean, it's their fault. After all, we said exactly what we meant. However, what the person on the receiving end heard or understood was quite different.

It is not anyone's fault! This is just one of the ways the communication process can go wrong. When we are communicating, what we say passes through several different layers of the way we feel (our emotions), the way we look (facial expressions), our vocal variety (tone, inflection, volume), and our body language. Communication is only seven percent verbal and ninety-three percent nonverbal. The nonverbal components are made up of body language (fifty-five percent) and tone of voice (thirty-eight percent).

Dramatic changes to our personal and professional lives are in our future because of the coronavirus, and these changes are being called the "new normal." In this new normal, relationships will be more critical than ever. Even the physical distance (six feet) that we maintain from each other has changed the way we relate to each other. However, communication is still the basis for all relationships, whether it happens face to face or virtual.

All communication consists of content and feelings. The content is based on the words we use, and the feeling is expressed through our nonverbal cues. Whenever there is a difference between the message's content and emotion, confusion is created. For example, say you are angry about something. Someone says, "Good morning" to you, and you respond with your "Good morning." Unconsciously you may have conveyed to the other party that you did not want to speak, or you do not particularly care for them, but that was not your intent. Even though the greeting was neutral or positive from your point of view, the listener may have interpreted it as negative. How do we get people to understand us? Think back, when was the last time you were misunderstood personally or professionally; how did you react? We have all been there.

In the most important personal relationship of my life, communication was a big problem. It appeared that the listener often misunderstood my words. My mother and I would argue repeatedly. One day, I asked, "Why is it that you frequently misinterpret what I say?" Her response was, "It's your facial expressions, your body language, and your tone of voice. If you want people to listen to you, then you need to listen to them, and you need to learn how to communicate better." When I think back, she used a lot of nonverbal communication to emphasize her point! Her comments returned to me later in life and caused me to question what was happening to me in the boardroom.

In an especially important strategizing meeting, my department was assigned the task of coming up with a program to be implemented throughout the company. Each one of us had to present our idea. I presented what I thought was a brilliant plan. When I looked around the table to see how it was accepted, I saw looks of disinterest. Why wasn't my idea heard? What amazed me was someone else had the same idea; they presented it differently, and they were applauded.

After that incident, I started analyzing my relationships with my colleagues, and I began comparing it to the relationships I saw between my other colleagues. I could see the difference in the way we communicated with each other, the difference in the relationships, and the different communication patterns in the boardroom. What I observed was the use of what I now know as effective communication.

Allow me to share with you the definition of effective communication. It is a two-way information sharing process that involves one person sending a message that is easily understood by the receiving person. Or, to put it in plain English, when you say something, the listener understands exactly what you mean. Effective communication determines how our voices are being heard.

The power behind a positive personal or professional relationship is effective communication. Good relationships cannot exist without proper communication. The way you communicate can make or break your personal and professional relationships. Effective communication can help you find the right way to express your feelings to your significant other. It can assist you in landing that sought-after job or securing that much-desired contract. The way you communicate can make people happy, sad, angry, bored, interested, etc. People judge you by how you communicate. Communicating effectively with finesse and diplomacy is not a gift that some people are born with. It is a skill that can be learned, practiced, and mastered.

There are internal and external barriers to effective communication. When these barriers are identified and removed, our communication skills improve. Some examples of internal barriers are poor listening skills, distractions, our attitude toward a person, or the information; our emotions including fear, mistrust, past experiences; and lack of common experiences. Having poor listening skills causes a major internal barrier. Listening is the ability to receive and interpret messages in the communication process correctively. Listening is the key to effective communication.

Without the ability to listen effectively, messages can be misunderstood. Effective listening is a skill that supports all

3

positive relationships. Distractions such as worry stress, anxiety, depression, sickness, hunger, pain, daydreams, and anticipation of upcoming events are examples that diminish your level of concentration. When listening to someone speaking, we may be thinking of how we are going to respond, while the other person is talking.

We pretend we are listening when what we are doing is creating our ideas and just waiting for the person to stop speaking so we can respond. Therefore, we are not actively listening. We may also be thinking of other things subconsciously.

How often have thoughts such as "What am I going to wear tomorrow?" or "It's getting late; I need to go to the store" or "I hope I will be able to finish that report in time" crossed your mind? At such times, we are distracted and are not giving our full attention to the conversation or speech. Our internal self-dialogue keeps us from focusing on the message. In other words, we are not actively listening to the speaker. We can minimize this internal barrier by focusing on the speaker, maintaining eye contact, and listening carefully. When we are not actively paying attention to the speaker, the result can be that we are making assumptions and coming up with conclusions about the speaker's message that might not be accurate.

There can be considerable room for misunderstanding between what the speaker intends to say, what the speaker says, and what the listener hears. One way to practice active listening is to concentrate on what the other person is saying and wait until they are finished talking before responding. Listen to learn and restate and share back information with the speaker to resolve any misunderstanding.

If the subject matter is emotionally charged, there can be a disconnect between the speaker and the listener. The listener may experience fear or mistrust, or the subject matter may bring up negative past experiences. When you are engrossed in your emotions, you tend to have trouble listening to others and understanding the message. If you are angry, resentful, or even happy or excited, you may be too preoccupied with emotions to receive the intended message.

Emotional intelligence is the ability to recognize our emotions and those of others and use that information to guide our communication process. Your ability to manage your feelings—knowing and understanding your emotions, overcoming stress, increasing your ability to read social cues, understanding what triggers you emotionally, and controlling your reactions—is a measure of your emotional intelligence.

Emotional intelligence consists of four key attributes: self-awareness, self-regulation, social awareness, and empathy. Self-awareness is the ability to know your emotions and what effect they have on the way you communicate. Self-regulation is the ability to think before you act or speak. Social awareness is the ability to manage relationships by finding common ground and building rapport. Empathy is understanding and appreciating the emotions, needs, and concerns of others and using that information to guide your behavior.

As you begin to understand how an increased awareness of emotional intelligence impacts the way you communicate verbally and nonverbally, you will be better equipped to handle how you respond in a variety of situations, and also better understand what others are talking to you about and why. Emotional intelligence is not something inborn; however, there are several ways to develop emotional intelligence.

Here are some ways to develop emotional intelligence. When we have a negative emotional reaction to something, it can be because we have unresolved issues. When you are experiencing negative emotions, calm down, and think about why you are experiencing them. It is usually helpful to write down the feelings you are experiencing and the possible reasons for them. Other ways to improve self-awareness are to write down your strengths and weaknesses when it comes to communication. Pay attention to what bothers you about other people. The behavior which annoys you may be a reflection of yourself. Ask yourself if you do some version of that disturbing behavior.

Pause and take a few moments of reflection. Ask yourself what you are trying to achieve through communication, and how you can change if you are not getting the desired results. It may be helpful to ask someone whose opinion you value to tell you how you come across to other people. Your self-regulation can improve by reinterpreting the conditions that can help change your emotional response to it. Rather than looking at a situation with a negative mindset, look at it again with a positive mindset. Practice staying calm under pressure by repeating a mantra until you feel yourself calming down—practice viewing challenges as opportunities.

Observe people in different situations. Notice how they respond and react and try to tune in to their emotions. Your ability to tune into their feelings will increase your ability to bond with other people. Find common ground and build rapport. Be interested in people. Remember their names and be aware of your body language. Biases interfere with developing empathy. Examples are gender, racial, and age biases, appearance, etc. Examine your preferences and think about why you have them. More than likely, you will find they are often based on stereotypes rather than personal experience or actual knowledge of an individual.

We may feel that the person speaking is unqualified to talk about a subject matter. Or we may have a preconceived bias about the content. Our standards and values can make it challenging to listen to the views of a speaker whose views or opinions are different from ours. Often, we form judgments of people, which leads to misjudgments.

When we stereotype a person, we become less objective and, therefore, are less likely to listen effectively. Focus on looking at people as individuals, instead of focusing on stereotypes to define people. Think about relating to people on a more personal, individual level, and try looking at things from the other person's point of view. As we can see, emotional intelligence plays a vital role in connecting with others and improving effective communication.

External barriers also affect communication. We do not always have control over these obstacles, which take place outside of the body and the mind. Examples of external barriers which can obstruct communication can include visual cues (nonverbal communication); noise and the environment; language and cultural differences; and time restrictions and mode of communication.

Nonverbal communication is virtually anything that sends an idea from one person to another without the use of words. Nonverbal communication plays a crucial role in effective communication. Body language is every bit as important as the words you say and how you say them. Whatever your body language is when you are speaking, the listener mimics the feeling they get from you.

The key components of body language include gestures, posture, facial expressions, eye contact, and vocal variety. Gestures are movements made with body parts (e.g., hands, arms, fingers, head, and legs), and they may be voluntary or involuntary. Arm gestures can be interpreted in several ways. Sometimes body language does not match the talking points and can cause confusion and mistrust. Understanding how to read and interpret body language can be extremely helpful in determining what another person's words mean and will impact your success at communicating effectively.

These are a few examples of familiar gestures and what they portray. Sitting or standing with arms folded across the chest usually signifies being defensive, resistant, stubborn, or angry. Arms open and palms up usually mean welcome and openness. When you touch your chin with your hand, it usually means that you are thinking about the information you are receiving, and you are evaluating it. If the person listening is doing this while you are speaking to them, they are taking you seriously enough to consider what you are saying. Head nodding lets the listener know that you are paying attention or agreeing with the speaker. As far as posture is concerned, standing up straight portrays confidence.

People watch your facial expressions during conversations and take cues about how they are supposed to react or feel from the looks on your face. An excellent communicator pays attention to micro-expressions, which are facial expressions that occur within a fraction of a second. The definition of a micro-expression is the natural result of a voluntary and an involuntary emotional response both occurring simultaneously and conflicting with one another. Microexpressions are extremely brief facial expressions that happen in about 1/25th of a second. They are an involuntary reaction that exposes a person's genuine emotions and occurs when you are trying to hold back your feelings. Microexpressions are present in everyone, often without their knowledge.

The seven basic micro expressions are happiness, sadness, surprise, disgust, anger, fear, and contempt. When you see someone showing a microexpression, it usually means that they are trying to conceal something from you. Let me give you an example. You greet a person, and they say to you that they are happy to meet you; however, in a split second, a look goes across their face that says just the opposite. If you learn to spot these micro-expressions, you can gain an advantage in any type of interaction.

Your eyes, eye movement, eyebrows, and mouth play a vital role in showing sadness, happiness, fear, anger, excitement, frustration boredom, interest, confidence, wonder, aggressiveness, and uncertainty. Have you ever spoken with someone who did not look directly at you? What did you think? Practicing good eye contact is an essential skill for effective communication. Maintaining eye contact with someone you are talking to displays that you are interested in them and in what they have to say. Eye contact is a powerful way to make a person feel recognized, understood, and validated.

The way you use your voice is also an essential tool in using effective communication. Vocal variety, when speaking, is a way to communicate your thoughts and intentions by changing the sound of your voice using different speeds and tones. Having a range of vocal variety helps keep the listener engaged and conveys your meaning, feelings, and emphasis. Each time you speak, you include your mind, body, and voice in connecting with your listener. Expressive speaking enhances communication, and there is an art to it. You can learn to use pitch, tone, volume, and rate to communicate with expression and emotion.

Pitch refers to the modulation of your voice while speaking (the highs and lows). An excellent communicator varies the pitch of his/her voice to express different emotions. A monotone voice is challenging to listen to because it is hard to maintain any interest in what you are saying. A sing-song sound when speaking is challenging to listen to because of the repeated variations in tone and pitch. The key is to find a pitch pattern between these two extremes.

The tone of your voice should convey a sense of friendliness. In an article by Greg Zlevor titled *The Power of Tone*, he notes that sincerity, enthusiasm, compassion, attention, concern, warmth, self-confidence, and authority cannot be feigned. Your listener will be affected by your tone, whether you or they are aware of it. When there is a difference between what the speaker is saying and the sound of their voice, people will trust what they perceive as the meaning in the tone rather than the actual words.

Volume is how loud or soft your speaking voice is, and how quickly or slowly you speak. Both are important in that varying your volume and rate helps to reflect mood changes and emphasizes essential points. It is useful to utilize the following vocal techniques: use loud and fast for impact, loud and slow for emphasis, low and fast to keep your listener engaged, and low and slow to express emotion. Remember, people may hear your words, but they listen and react to all the qualities of your voice.

These examples of vocal variety techniques allow your voice to be heard by your listeners.

Cultural differences can be an external barrier to effective communication. Culture plays an essential role in determining the style of communication. The culture in which people live socially impacts the way they communicate with others. Cultural barriers in communication happen when communication experiences occur between two different cultural backgrounds.

We often encounter cultural barriers in everyday life. Different cultures have different meanings of words, signs, symbols, habits, behaviors, and gestures. Our world of communication has become more global; therefore, it is particularly important to become as aware as possible when speaking to people whose culture is different from our own. Good communication can happen between people from different cultures. We must accept cultural differences with an open mind.

Cross-cultural communication involves understanding how culturally distinct individuals communicate with each other and how they endeavor to communicate across cultures. Language is considered a critical barrier to cross-cultural communication. One of the main principles of effective cross-cultural communication is that there is no judgment. Because verbal communication is vital in every context, being aware of the correct meaning of words can prevent misunderstandings and conflicts. Body language and gestures are also elements of the cultural barrier.

The following are a few interesting hand gestures that mean different things in different cultures. The thumbs-up sign in America means good or great, but in Iraq or Iran, it is an insult. In America, the hand sign for okay means money in Japan but is a rude gesture in Brazil. Looking at your watch in America can mean you just want to know the time, or you are in a hurry. But in the Arabic culture, it is considered rude. Other barriers include negative stereotypes and values and beliefs that are different from our own. In our ever-increasing global environment, we must learn about other cultures and their norms, accept different cultures, and, if you are in doubt, ask questions.

A top concern for many businesses is internal and external communication. More and more companies and organizations have diversified environments. The workforce may include people from different cultures, races, religions, ages, and gender. Effective communication in the workplace pays dividends throughout the organization. It can improve worker productivity, increase employee job satisfaction, have a positive effect on absenteeism, and improve professional relationships. It also helps in building productive teams. Leaders who are skilled communicators can motivate, inspire, and instill trust in their team and employees. If your organization or business is having communication challenges, you should identify and evaluate the issues. You may need to invest in a consultant or coach to solve the problems.

I have shared the definition of effective communication, provided examples of ineffective communication, discussed internal and external barriers, and explained the role of emotional intelligence, and the importance of body language. I sincerely hope that I have given you valuable information that you will utilize in improving your communication skills. We all want our voices to be heard!

—JHFortman & Associates, LLC, President

PART 2

Personal And Business Financial Literacy Keys For Success

CHAPTER 2

MANAGING THROUGH A FINANCIAL DOWNTURN
HOW TO SURVIVE IN A FAMINE

By Dr. Joseph Webb III, CKA, CRFA, CLTC

I want to tell a little story about how the decisions we make affect our bottom line all the time. My people, we are in a famine. I want to talk about some of the things that we can do to manage ourselves through this modern-day global famine. In my spiritual wisdom, I think that God was trying to show us what a famine was in the 2000 bursting of the Technology Bubble, in 2001, after the bombing of the Twin Towers in New York (9/11). And, of course, who could forget the Housing Bubble that burst in 2008 during the Great Recession.

I came into the financial services business in 2000/2001. Yes, right after two major market swings. People felt sorry for me. My family, friends, and colleagues tried to discourage me from leaving my very secure job as an electronics technician with a very prominent company. Had I stayed with that company, I would have worked there thirty years as of September 2020.

As a tech guy, I lived during the nineties as a consumer watching computers enter the homes of millions of families for the first time in American history. One entered my home in 1993 at the cost of $4200! Yes. My engineer coworker built for me an Intel 486 maxed out computer with all the bells and whistles. He assured me that I would not have to purchase another computer again! I am sure he believed it, and so did I. Then, two years later, Windows 95 put my computer on obsolescence death row.

I also lived during the technology bubble as a technician who worked on the hardware of computers along with about forty other stock market 401k day-trading technicians who would have bet on their mothers' lives that we were in a time that would never change! "We will always need technology" was the phrase of the day. Millions of Americans felt the same way. Computers were coming off the store shelves in droves. Advertisements were all over our TVs to invest in computer technology, hardware, storage centers, etc. The internet with the .com companies entered our homes in mass numbers.

What we did not know was that we had overspent and bought high. I did it. The efficiency of unnecessary upgrades every couple of years was lost and unsustainable. The technology stock market bubble burst happened! Most retirement plan 401ks lost half their value. Many jobs were lost. Computers today are seventy-five percent cheaper because of this catastrophic, yet innovative, time in our history.

Now, the 2008 real estate bubble that burst was not amazing. No, it was not. What was amazing was watching America do the same thing with real estate as they did with technology. They jumped in with both hands and feet, not realizing that we were heading over a different financial cliff with the same painful landing. I taught, and I lectured, I preached at many venues to no avail, feeling like Paul Revere, "The Great Recession is coming! The real estate recession is coming!" What we did not know was that the housing market's dramatic annual value increases were unsustainable in many areas with a modest income, employment, and industries. Retirement plans were devalued, jobs were lost, and homes were at least fifty percent cheaper, i.e., the Great Recession.

Doesn't this sound familiar? We bought high, sold low, instead of buying low and selling high. We failed to use the old cliché that has been around since the market's creation in the 1850s, BUY LOW, SELL HIGH. We also failed to use a principle that has been around since the beginning of time. Diversify, diversify, diversify. "But divide your investments among many places, for you do not know what risks might lie ahead" (Ecclesiastes 11:2, NLT).

In every economic downturn, banks play a major role in the movement of money. That includes commerce, debt, and consumerism. The banks overinflated, then stalled the economy, causing the 2008 economic downturn by losing trust in one another. National banks typically lend to regional banks who lend to local banks, and this was simply not happening! This gigantic void manifested because banks were lending out forty times the money they had on their books. What does forty times zero equal? The normal leveraging allowed in banking is eight to ten times the amount you have in deposits. Wouldn't you say they overextended themselves just a little bit?

Overextending meant that you could not go anywhere to finance anything. During economic contractions, it does not matter what credit score you have. In today's financial crisis, the global COVID-19 pandemic, car dealerships are allowing you to purchase a car and delay making payments for up to six months. In the 2009's Global Great Recession, you could buy a car and get the second one free. Yes, an auto BOGO (buy one get one). But you had to purchase the first one with cash, no financing. The travesty was even deeper than that. If banks are not moving money, that means no cash is flowing, which prevents companies from producing, hiring, and paying their bills.

Now, imagine what happens when the cash stops flowing in your household. For some, that could mean one paycheck, but for most, it was equivalent to the loss of a job, where unemployment was at an all-time high of nine percent (in the Great Recession). Today (COVID-19 pandemic), unemployment is eighteen percent as of April 30, 2020. Nothing is coming in to pay your bills or sustain any lifestyle. Now, multiply that times a million people. Yes, at least that many were affected, and at the same time! It gets more exciting. I have mentioned this a few times, but I am not sure if you caught this. Did you know that our economic system is global and interconnected?

Have you ever heard the term New World Order? It is already here, alive and kicking. It is where the world's economic system is under one economy with different currencies and valuations of them. When the US markets shut down in 2008, within weeks, many of our world economies had to shut down as well. Look at our current global COVID-19 pandemic. Can you see the similarities? We are all interconnected by computers. When one country struggles, the global economy struggles. Some catch a cold, while others get the flu.

Before every recession, market downturns, or famine of any kind, there is always prosperity. Great prosperity. There is a story in the Good Book that talks about the seven years of great prosperity in the land of Egypt. And afterward, there were seven years of famine that ravaged the land, so severe that the memories of "The Good Years" were erased (Genesis 41:28-32, NLT paraphrased).

Can you see the similarities between the technology bubble of the nineties, the real estate bubble of the 2000s, and the economic record-setting growth of the past decade? The nineties were great years of opportunity to invest in real estate and manage the risk of our investments in technology and the stock market.

This sector and time are what brought me into this field. I was purchasing properties in the nineties because of a good friend and mentor that taught me some things while in the military. Yes, I was fortunate then, which is why I am paying it forward, as they say. Unfortunately, the closest that most come to mentorship is a coworker, a neighbor, the barbershop, or the beauty salon. Then there was the Real Estate Bubble that took place from 2005 to 2008. We simply didn't know how to research what was happening in the mortgage lending world of subprime loans: adjustable-rate mortgages, interest-only loans, no DOC loans (which means no documentation), and stated income loans.

Most of these loans were awarded to people with credit challenges and without providing the information necessary to support a successful outcome. That is right; no one has bad credit—just challenges to overcome. The hurting thing was the lack of real estate tax assessment knowledge in newly built communities. People did not research the tax rolls in newly developed communities. Neither the developers nor the lenders educated the borrower that most tax assessments were about a year behind and based on the appraised price of your house when you purchased it, not based on your neighbor's house!

In most cases, this raised homeowners' mortgage payments twenty to thirty percent per month the following year. Opportunities turned disastrous for more than one million homeowners. The bursting of the Real Estate Bubble affected large business chains, like Circuit City, DHL Shipping, and Bennigan's Restaurants. These businesses, along with many others, even globally, no longer exist today because of the Great Recession.

Most people missed the growth of the stock market from the last decade (2009-2019). I taught, lectured, and preached at many venues to no avail, feeling like Paul Revere, "The market is growing, the market is soaring; get off the sidelines!" Of course, you know what happened. The market bottomed out in March 2009, and more than quadrupled in ten years! Yes, the market bottomed out and quadrupled in ten years. According to Finance Yahoo.com, the Dow Jones Industrial Average (DJIA) bottomed out at a closing price of 6,547 on 3/09/2009 during the Great Recession and peaked at 29,440 on 2/14/2020 as the global COVID-19 pandemic reached our shores. With the downturn of the stock market, since this chapter was written, the market still more than tripled since 2009.

Unfortunately, there are going to be a lot of small businesses that will not survive this global COVID-19 pandemic famine. As with the other famines, life will not be the same as we once knew it. Can you see the patterns? We have had years of abundance but have failed to take advantage of them. Between the last two bull and bear markets, the government has had to pump almost four trillion dollars into our economy, yes trillion with a "t." During the Great Recession, the government implemented the stimulus ARRA package money (American Recovery and Reinvestment Act of 2009). With the COVID-19 pandemic, The CARES Act

(Coronavirus Aid, Relief, and Economic Security) were both injected into the economy in April 2020.

Now, I am not here pointing fingers. I am just merely stating this fact: failing to plan is what the masses do, which leads to one thing, like it or not—planned failure. When we fail to save and do not plan, as it says in the Good Book, the government must intervene, which puts us in a dependent, needy, inferior position in this land of milk and honey. We are in a famine. With that said, we have a government that is also needy, dependent, and inferior. We have an unbalanced budget, an out-of-control twenty-plus trillion-dollar deficit, and a system that prints money while producing little to no gross domestic product (GDP).

Sadly, a significant part of our gross domestic product (GDP) is spending and consumerism. Yes, from the White House to your house, we live in a system that is run and based on consumerism, debt, and interest rates. The Federal Reserve lowered interest rates eleven times in 2005 to stimulate the economy, and it has not been the same since. In March 2020, the Feds lowered the rate to less than one percent, another first in American history. We do not want to see a negative interest rate because it could have a negative effect on America's credit rating. Yes, America and all countries have a credit rating. So, if the White House is in debt with credit challenges, this may raise concern for you having your credit challenges.

The Good Book says, "Don't agree to guarantee another person's debt or put up security for someone else. If you cannot pay it, your very bed will be snatched out from under you" (Proverbs 22:26-27). Take heed to these words of wisdom. You, your children, and your children's children financial future depend on your financial mindset.

Here is a riddle for you. Can you guess who the number one producing country in the world is? The number one country in the world that purchases U.S. debt (T-Bonds, T-Bills, and T-Notes) and the number one country that makes ninety percent of everything we have? The answer: CHINA, CHINA, and

CHINA. They make our Aspirin, certain vaccines, and even our Christmas bulbs! So, if the White House does not care about U.S. production, why would they care about production in your house? Things that make you say hmmm.

Let's talk about answers. What can we do about the global famine and our household famine? It all starts with a new mindset, a shift from a constant reactionary being to that of a consistent "proactionary" being. We cannot just freeze up and do nothing like a deer in headlights waiting for something to happen. Guess what? Something is always happening to you, like the deer, or through you, like the power of flowing water.

Today, in 2020, because of this global COVID-19 pandemic, many people are dealing with loneliness and bouts of depression because of the mandatory stay-at-home orders, self-quarantines, and self-distancing. During these times, we should be learning more about our Maker. We should be reading and learning more about ourselves and using our technology to communicate. We should focus on creation, not destruction. The mind is a terrible thing to waste. The Good Book says, "He is like a tree planted by streams of water that yields its fruit in its season, and its leaf does not wither. In all that he does, he prospers" (Psalms 1:3). Take action to obtain knowledge, wisdom, and wealth.

We have got to watch what we put into our "mind system" as in your brain. Reality shows are not our reality. They are someone else's reality. Soap operas are the same. Why are we focusing on other people's lives? Instead, we should be focusing on the days of our lives. Time waits for no one and is the most precious thing that we have. The things we read do matter. Are we learning things that empower or impair our minds? As you have seen, the Good Book is a great place to start. The same goes for what we listen to, our vocabulary, and our circle of people with whom we congregate. The Good Book says that "Iron sharpens iron and without vision, the people perish!" It is time for us to ride the wave to prosperity. That will only happen when we are sick and tired of chasing the wave of exhaustion or being drowned by the wave of overwhelm.

Empowerment and dominion! It is time to get control of our finances! We have money, and it is merely blindly allocated in all the wrong places. Sometimes, it is in someone else's pockets! We must change our attitude about money and have respect for what it can do in our lives. No, it does not grow on trees, but money works twenty-four hours a day, seven days a week. It takes no breaks and does not discriminate, being green in color.

We must become producers and not consumers. Producers work, create, and make things happen. Consumers sit around, waste time, and miss opportunities! The Good Book says, "He who works his land will have abundant food, but the one who chases fantasies will have his share of poverty" (Proverbs 12:11).

Lotto winners are losers. Ninety percent go broke within eighteen months. Only one ticket wins, with a one-in-millions chance of that happening. Yet, I have seen people spend one hundred dollars per week on lotto. Maybe your get rich plan is betting on the horses, betting on sports, or gambling in the casinos. These pitfalls are not places to plant seeds if you genuinely want a harvest.

My people we have got work to do! Our salary and wage system, when it comes to work and money, has not kept up with inflation, which is another issue. Back when I was in the third grade, I did a book report on my dad (now deceased), who was an inspector with the Chevrolet/General Motors plant in Parma, Ohio, a suburb of Cleveland. He made $27,000 per year. Our house cost $18,000, and Cadillacs were $12,000. Easy math, better living, better wages, the money went much further back then than it does today, and my dad's job could not be inherited or willed to our family. So, when he died, our financial lifestyle died. I was in high school and the oldest of four siblings.

The government has not and will not put anything in place that will empower you. Right now, every generation starts from zero. What a tragedy. As it is, our children did not ask to be here, and we top it off by not providing them with a financial starter kit. We must save and put something away for them. The way we handle money affects not only our children but our children's children. Yes, the next two generations. With that, what we see today should be no surprise. The Good Book says, "Be sure you know the condition of your flocks, give careful attention to your herds; for riches do not endure forever, and a crown is not secure for all generations" (PR 27:23-24). Add generational wealth to your vocabulary, and it will become your new family legacy.

Learn the many facets of how money truly works. Money is a mystery in and of itself. Money is a tool, a vision, an idea, that depending on what it is attached to, can mean different things. Our tax system has many ways that you can file for your income tax returns. There are many different types of income. Most of us know the JOB W2 wage income. But what about business income, passive income, residual income, royalties, dividends, before tax, after-tax, and tax-advantaged income? There are many ways to save money using different vehicles, including retirement plans like IRAs, 401ks, SDLI, Roths, and compound interest and distribution rules like the rule of 72 and the four percent rule. The concepts of debt and credit can be complicated. Remember this saying: "The bold print giveth and the small print taketh away!" Not knowing these things can cause us to waste tens of thousands of dollars over our lifetime. You must know your bottom line and count the total cost of your actions.

So, what can we do to build that financial house, that starter kit? Let us start by saving a cash reserve. Having a cash reserve will take care of our needs first, provide security for those rainy days, and of course, let us not forget financial opportunities and wants. There should be three to six months of cash reserves based on your budget, also known as a monthly spending plan. We must understand what is coming in and going out before we can determine that three to six-month number. No, my friend, cash reserves do not include credit cards. The aim is cash. The Good Book says, "Those who love pleasure become poor; those who love wine and luxury will never be rich" (Proverbs 21:17). We must break the yoke of bondage and change our way of doing things.

Asset protection is next, and it starts with you. Yes, you are an asset. Your life has value and must be protected; hence, life insurance. Depending on the type (term or permanent), and what you can afford, life insurance can have many living benefits like college planning and retirement planning. It can also have a hybrid type of long-term care, and the best benefit is a concept known as "the infinite banking concept." The infinite banking concept is a unique wealth-building leveraging strategy.

Next, you must protect your income with some type of disability income insurance, short or long term, group, or individual. Long term care (LTC) insurance is needed because we are living longer. Many different strategies can provide an affordable type of LTC.

A will or trust must is a tool that is available to provide that last love letter to your children. Families, unfortunately, tend to break up without having them in place, leaving family members to fight over assets. The definition of probate is the process of validating a deceased person's will. In plain English, a will is a must!

Finally, let's talk about that permanent vacation, better known as retirement. Retirement should be the most exciting part of our starter kit, but unfortunately, it is the most neglected. Only five out of every 100 people retire with wealth or some level of independence. Eight out of ten people seek employment within five years after retiring, realizing that although they were physically tired, they were not fiscally ready to retire.

The permanent vacation gets neglected by the trips to Disney World, cruising, and trips to different countries around the world all in the same year. Okay, maybe not all three, but two out of three. I have seen this happen and with a substantial price to pay by not saving enough and having to work longer or be taken care of by other family members. Not Good!

My people, we are underfunding our company, city, county, state, and government-sponsored retirement plans, especially if they are matching the amount you are saving. Employer matching could double the amount you are saving monthly for retirement. That is free money; what an incentive! We must prepare by knowing what our retirement income number needs to be, which is how much money we should have saved by the time we are ready to retire so that our funds will sustain us through retirement.

Most of us are taught how to get to retirement, but not how to financially live through retirement. The future of our Social Security and Medicare benefits are changing for the worse right before our eyes. The Tax Cut and Jobs Act of 2017 has made Social Security even more taxable, and Medicare costs no longer have a cap on the premiums. Why not? In the big picture, by the end of 2026, there will be more people retired than working! That is only six years from now. Pay attention my people. Our purchasing a new home close to retirement without proper planning can have a compounding effect.

The Good Book says, "For who would begin the construction of a building without first calculating the cost to see if there's enough money to finish it? Otherwise, you might complete only the foundation before running out of money, and everyone will laugh at you. They would say, 'There's the person who started that building and couldn't finish it'" (Luke 14:28-30). "However, by wisdom, a house is built, and through understanding, it is established; through knowledge, its rooms are filled with rare and beautiful treasures" (Proverbs 24:3-4). What a beautiful ending.

Seek counsel to gain knowledge and understanding. Take action to succeed, and with many advisors, you will avoid famines and manage your way through financial downturns. It is a dangerous thing ever to think you know everything. A know-it-all person will continue to make unwise decisions, stepping on the famine mines to poverty. Remember, you have the power of choice! Get knowledge, wisdom, and wealth. Peace, love, and blessings!

—Dr. Joseph Webb III

CHAPTER 3

IT TAKES A TRIBE TO RAISE A VILLAGE

By Michael Perkins

P icture a network of thousands or perhaps millions of entrepreneurs from thriving villages and prosperous communities around the globe who come together to collaborate and share their knowledge, wisdom, and expertise. Imagine these same entrepreneurs buying from one another online and at local retail stores. How would your life be different if you had access to such a community where dollars easily circulated, and information was easily shared?

Now, imagine a prosperous community with thriving grocery stores, barbershops, beauty salons, clothing stores, movie theaters, and hotels, all being reduced to rubble in the blink of an eye. Imagine no longer. There is documentation that such a prosperous community existed. The destruction of that community is a part of the history of Black Wall Street.

In 1921, Black Wall Street, an area located in Tulsa, Oklahoma, was considered the wealthiest black community in America. In the Greenwood section of Tulsa, "Every dollar that came into the black community would change hands at least 16 times and sometimes up to a year before it left the community," according to Jeff Dawkins, co-chair of Illinois Black Wall Street.

Fast forward to May 31, 2020, almost 100 years after the decimation of Black Wall Street on May 31, 1921. Once again, black businesses are being destroyed as we speak. However, black businesses are not the only businesses that are being destroyed. Millions of companies across America are on life support due to the devastating, insidious coronavirus (COVID-19) that is wreaking death upon people and devastation on businesses throughout the world.

During this latest wave of devastation to businesses across America, I am collaborating with other socially conscious entrepreneurs to fund 600 new businesses by May 31, 2021. We will do this in honor of the 600 Black Wall Street businesses that were destroyed in 1921. Also, because I am concerned for the businesses that are being lost due to the COVID-19 virus, we will collaborate to assist 10,000 existing businesses in gaining access to capital to rebuild their companies.

O.W. Gurley, a wealthy black landowner, acknowledged as the first black business owner in Greenwood (Tulsa), Oklahoma, in 1906, was known for lending money to people who wanted to start a business. Dawkins supports the idea of communities being self-reliant and emphasizes that we should use our funds to start the rebuilding process as the earlier trailblazers did on Black Wall Street. In the early 1920s, J.B. Stradford, an outspoken businessman and the owner of the largest black-owned luxury hotel in the country, believed that blacks could make more considerable economic progress if they pooled their money. I agree because collaborative economics is one of the core values of Tribal Wealth United. We will use our funds to start the rebuilding process; however, we will also leverage other funding sources to raise capital.

The need for business owners and entrepreneurs to collaborate has never been greater than at the current time. As I draft this chapter, we are in the seventh week of a healthcare pandemic that is wreaking economic chaos on both Wall Street and main street. Tens of thousands of small businesses are ceasing day to day operations, while others are closing their doors permanently. The spread of the coronavirus must decrease until the health crisis subsides. Over thirty million employees are filing for unemployment compensation. At the same time, the assets of America's most wealthy citizens have risen by over $300 billion.

The federal government has issued paychecks to some individuals for $1,200 to keep the economy moving and has provided $350 billion in funding for small business owners, which was absorbed in two weeks by the largest of the small businesses. Those businesses were first in line to receive the funding.

The funds were provided on a first-come, first-served basis. While the larger businesses had pre-existing relationships with the banks, black, brown, and underfunded entrepreneurs, only had pre-existing health conditions.

As we go into the eighth week of the COVID-19 pandemic, another $310 billion in small business funding has been approved by the federal government. Additional funding is needed, but if the past is prologue, many small businesses that are in dire need of the funds required to keep their doors open will never receive it. Businesses that may not benefit could be; barbershops, nail salons, beauty shops, and cafes. Even home remodeling contractors, landscapers, and truckers may not benefit. These businesses are profoundly impacted by COVID-19 and are now in need of funding more than ever before.

Leadership for a Hopeful People in Times of Normalcy, Crises, and Chaos

Throughout the years, our country has flourished or floundered because of leadership or lack of leadership at the helm. In the Industrial Age, the standard of living of most Americans increased significantly in comparison to that of other families in the Western world. During that same period, the wealth gap between the elite and the majority of Americans grew exponentially. This massive redistribution of wealth led to greater wealth inequality. As a direct result, the policies were set by political leaders in association with business leaders and adhered to by a population of people with an insufficient level of financial knowledge.

The Digital Revolution has put more technology into the hands of humanity than ever before. However, the wealth gap continues to grow. The challenge of overcoming this growing wealth inequality is more insurmountable because now two gaps must be closed. In addition to closing the gap in financial literacy, now a more significant number of people must close the difference in their digital literacy.

The development of social sharing sites in the 21st century has disrupted the way we share personal information with our friends, the way we build new relationships online, and even how we select our political leaders. On the economic front, social sharing and e-commerce sites have also disrupted the way we do business. Blockbuster lost out to Netflix in the movie rental space because they failed to develop an online platform. Thousands of brick and mortar stores lost out to Amazon because they were unable to build e-commerce sites. Now that Amazon is the dominant platform in the e-commerce industry, small businesses have a difficult time carving out their piece of the pie unless they can create or share a platform. Doing so will allow them consistent and predictable ways to generate revenue. The good news is that Tribal Wealth United, in collaboration with other forward-thinking entrepreneurs, has created such a platform and is on a crusade to provide financial education and leadership development to motivated, likeminded people around the world. To be clear, we are at a transformational point that will alter the business landscape for decades going forward.

Some small businesses hope that the government will intercede on their behalf and institute policies that will ensure their survival. Other businesses will continue to do more of what they had been doing before the onset of COVID-19. They will work harder while doing more of the same as the solution for sustaining their business. On the other hand, some businesses will adapt to the changing new world order. These business owners realize that while battles are being fought for the consumer dollar on Main Street, there is a war being fought on the internet superhighway. The internet war leaves small business owners shut out on two fronts, and black businesses shut out on all fronts unless there is a collaborative response to the challenge of COVID-19. Join the challenge at tribalwealthunited.com.

Build a Business Around a System That Empowers You

In America, we live in a capitalistic society where everyone can choose their economic fate. However, that choice is undercut by societal norms and an educational system that does not prepare us for starting businesses or investing in assets that generate wealth. "It Takes a Tribe to Raise a Village" is a primer on how different tribes come together to collaborate and launch businesses, accumulate assets, and build sustainable communities.

One of my mentors, Dr. James Dentley, often says that when the student is ready, the teacher shows up. At a recent Business Accelerator conference hosted by Dr. James Dentley and Dr. Kara Scott Dentley in Oak Brook, Illinois, the teacher showed up: Sharon Lechter, co-author of the Rich Dad Poor Dad book with Robert Kiyosaki. In her presentation, Lechter pointed out a concept that I had heard many times before, but somehow this time, I received it. Lechter simply stated that "Cash flow from assets creates financial freedom." Yes, I finally had the key. "Cash flow from assets creates financial freedom." I could take that simple concept, put it in a bottle, and take it to market; however, if only it were that simple.

As I thought about creating assets from cash flow, I realized there was another question. That is, what is the best way to create cash flow? There are three ways to generate cash flow to create assets initially—# 1. You can find a job and work for someone else—# 2. You can find a side hustle or business opportunity and become self-employed—# 3. You can incorporate your own business and create your brand.

As you may suspect, the three options come with varying levels of risk and reward. The conventional wisdom is that you should start by working a "secure" corporate job to generate cash flow and save money while earning a guaranteed paycheck. In the gig economy, more people have taken to working side jobs to earn more cash to satisfy the needs of an on-demand marketplace.

The money from these "side hustles" often is used to supplement current income and fund their business startup. In the aftermath of COVID-19, I can say with great certainty that we will never again approach how we earn income based on the conventional wisdom of the last century.

Experts estimate that currently, we are near the midpoint in the pandemic, and forty million Americans are unemployed. Many of these people who are now in the unemployment line only had one stream of income, and that was their job. When they lost that lifeline, everything in their world turned upside down. There is a significant risk of having only one stream of income and one type of income. Employees are less secure, with only one stream of income. They have more security when they earn recurring revenue in addition to the linear income earned from jobs.

How to Build an Online Membership Business Using Collaborative Economics

The fastest and most effective method of generating consistent cash flow is to launch your own business, especially an online business. After researching various business trends and many different business models, I found that online education, particularly financial education, ranked extremely high regarding business trends. In researching many different business models, building an online membership network has proven to be the most effective business model to generate consistent and predictable income. There are online memberships that charge from $10 to $25,000 a month to join a community of likeminded people that deliver specific results for their members. Most memberships cost a minimum of $97 per month.

Besides allowing the owners of the site to earn consistent and predictable income, membership sites are popular for primarily four reasons. They solve problems for the people who join the tribe (membership). As an example, people join wellness memberships because they want to receive monthly tips on a diet or weight control. People join business development memberships because they want to receive monthly tips that will assist them in growing their business.

Secondly, membership sites are great for teaching members the step by step skills over time that will allow them to produce predictable results. Thirdly, membership sites offer great convenience and save members an enormous amount of time, because a large variety of content can be curated on one platform. Finally, an online membership site is an excellent platform for members to come together as a tribe and make a more significant impact. No one can do it alone. It takes a tribe to raise a village. Join us at tribalwealthunited.com to become a founding ambassador.

Four Keys to Using a Membership Site to Build an Online Business

1. **Rally Around a Great Cause:** A significant cause sparks every movement that captures the attention and arouses the imagination of a mass number of people. When people can identify with the purpose of the campaign, the movement will generate more interest and enthusiasm. As the excitement grows, so will the momentum, and growing memberships will follow. Never underestimate the power of a cause that can move people to action. As members and ambassadors of Tribal Wealth United, our motto is "No Family Left Behind," which we accomplish by providing financial education to consumers and providing access to capital to entrepreneurs and small business owners.

2. **Offer an Incentive or Loyalty Rewards Program to Affiliates:** All seven-figure internet businesses leverage the power of collaborating with affiliates to drive more traffic to their sites or their offers. We can all learn a lesson from the guys who are playing at the top when it comes to working together to generate leads and sales. However, many membership programs do not pay

affiliate commissions. So, when you find one that does, there is cause for celebration. It is even rarer for affiliates to receive income by referring other affiliates.

3. **Provide a Road Map that Leads to Predictable Results:** This is the key that makes membership sites the "Holy Grail" of online marketing. In most business models, you make a sale, and you do not get paid again until you make another sale. Membership sites allow you to get paid over and over again, month after month, because of the built-in subscription feature. However, most people will not continue to pay the subscription fee if they do not get results fast, and they will not pay it for long if they do not continue to see results. By providing a roadmap to success, it is much easier for members to stay focused and remain consistent. The roadmap gives members clarity on the action steps they should take and the milestones they should reach along their journey.

4. **Encourage Collaboration Between the Tribes:** It is the nature of tribes to stay to themselves, but in the new economy, it is more important for tribes to collaborate. The process of collaboration increases the long-term survival of all tribes.

Two Keys to Launching a Fast-Growing Six-Figure Membership Site

KEY #1: Get Clarity

Before launching your membership campaign, the first thing you absolutely must do is get clarity on these five points:

1. Who are you?
2. Your purpose.
3. Your tribe, your community, the people you serve.
4. The immediate result(s) that you get for your tribe.
5. The big payoff that your tribal members receive.

KEY #2: Follow a Road Map

The most crucial thing you can do for your tribe is to provide a road map to success, which includes guideposts along the way. For example, as members reach specific predetermined points on the path to success, guideposts indicate each member's current position of achievement while advancing toward the next milestone on their journey.

To start the journey, Guidepost #1 could read: This is for you if you want to maximize your influence and help others make a positive difference in the world. This is for you if you want to make a dollar while making a difference. This is for you if you are tired of being your own best-kept secret with exceptional value to share.

Guidepost #2 could read: At this point, you should have clarity on your identity, your big Why, and Who the people are that support and follow you and are attracted to your message and your vision. There should be at least three to five people who have joined your crusade.

Using a membership site to launch a six-figure business (if the membership program paid its members recurring income), Guidepost #3 on the road map would read something like this: At this point, you are collaborating with a team of three people which qualifies you as a leader. You are now qualified to earn recurring monthly income. Congratulations!

The 4th guidepost could read: You are off to a great start. Your business is paying for itself, and you are now generating enough cash flow to invest in your next asset or business.

By the time you reach the 9th Guidepost, you would have a secure business with multiple streams of income. You would have recurring income being financially free.

Shift

In the swirl of the pandemic, large retail stores, and other businesses without the benefit of visionary leadership to recognize profitable and sustainable trends have already started to file for bankruptcy. Retail giants like J. Crew with 500 plus stores, JC Penney with 865 stores, and upscale retailer Neiman Marcus, with forty-two stores, were among the first casualties. These business failures will produce a domino effect that will have a detrimental impact on the livelihood of thousands of employees. The demise of these businesses, and many to follow, are not all due to COVID-19. These businesses were holding on to old business models. The virus merely hastened the process of closure.

In addition to the tremendous human suffering, high mortality rates, and record unemployment, the COVID-19 pandemic has brought many painful truths to light. The fatal effects of income inequality have proven to be far more devastating to blacks than any other people. Poor health care, lack of access to nutritious food, and joblessness are factors that contribute to pre-existing conditions that make blacks susceptible to various diseases and viruses. Dr. Claude Anderson says that blacks were not impacted as much by high unemployment due to COVID-19 because black employment was low from the start. In an interview with Dr. Boyce Watkins, and Dr. Anderson pointed out that, "Blacks suffer more from joblessness than unemployment." Blacks are not employed at high levels in major urban areas because there is not a vast pool of businesses owned by blacks who will hire other blacks. Joblessness is not an economic formula for sustainability.

The entrepreneurs and investors who prosper in the aftermath of COVID-19 will be those who can grasp trends that embrace sustainability. Jeff Bezos, Warren Buffet, and BlackRock (the world's largest asset management corporation) are all positioned to put their money behind businesses that include sustainability as a core business proposition. According to an article by Ian Jenkins, dated May 6, 2020, sustainability is a "$30 trillion-plus megatrend." When speaking of sustainability, entrepreneurs such as Bezos, Buffet, and Gates are referring to climate change and green technology. Warren Buffet is famously known for saying, "Energy deregulation will be the largest transfer of wealth in history."

However, when you look at sustainability from a leadership perspective, there are three components to what or the triple bottom line—people, planet, and profit. When these investors look at sustainable trends, they are focused on providing solutions that will sustain the environment and increase profits.

The focus on what is being done to improve the lives of people in inner-city neighborhoods is a distant third. Amid all the chaos, there is a golden opportunity hiding in plain sight. The entrepreneurs who seize the moment and muster a plan to galvanize other socially conscious people to commit to investing in themselves and their communities will prosper.

In terms of raising the bar when it comes to sustainability, I would suggest that entrepreneurs increase their level of financial literacy. Learn what it takes to get access to business funding and corporate credit. Approximately two million small businesses will receive funding from the Paycheck Protection Program (PPP). Still, nearly twenty-eight million businesses will need funding. Many of these businesses will fail because the owners do not have access to enough resources to overcome the process of identifying and securing the best source of capital funding. They do not teach concepts of credit management and business funding in school.

There are only four states that require financial education in school, while there are thirty-seven states that require sex education. There is little wonder that both business owners and consumers lack the knowledge to consistently make sound financial decisions when it comes to managing cash flow, managing debt, accumulating assets, and preserving wealth.

To resolve this problem, we created an online network that will offer members the opportunity to collaborate to earn consistent and predictable income. The online network is a community of ambassadors that collaborates and shares referrals while building their respective tribes. The membership platform provides a roadmap to financial success by achieving preset milestones. Start your journey to financial freedom at tribalwealthunited.com.

Five Shifts to Change Your Life While Building a Sustainable Community

1. How You Think About Money
2. How You Earn/Create Money
3. How You Save Money
4. How You Invest Money
5. How You Spend Money

To learn how you can make these 5 SHIFTS join us at tribalwealthunited.com.

From Paycheck to Freedom

COVID-19 has initiated a reset in the business marketplace. Larger businesses are being bailed out once again because of their relationships with bankers who provide funding. The smaller companies will struggle and fail while the economy recovers. The fact of the matter is that good times and bad times, there will always be businesses that thrive, whether large or small.

The question is; what are those businesses and how does one access the opportunity to leverage those businesses. The most effective way to determine which companies will thrive in times of chaos and turmoil is to look at trends. In the process of researching current trends, I found two of the most profitable trends today are online coaching and financial education.

Online coaching is quickly developing into a vast industry, and the demand for financial coaches is skyrocketing. Nearly half of all existing financial advisors are over the age of fifty-five, and roughly one-third will retire over the next decade, according to Reuters, Feb 11, 2015. The pace has especially quickened over the last two years. You, too, can achieve financial freedom or become a financial coach. Join us at tribalwealthunited.com. Thank You!

—Michael Perkins
Founder, Tribal Wealth United

CHAPTER 4

PRINCIPLES, PRECEPTS, AND PROCESSES
BEING A GOOD STEWARD OF YOUR FINANCES

By Calvin W. Denson, Sr.

> And my God will meet all your needs according
> to the riches of His glory in Christ Jesus.
> (Philippians 4:19) NIV

As the coronavirus has affected you, think about how financially prepared you were for this pandemic. Are there things you might have been able to do to be better prepared? In the above scripture, Peter stated, "God will meet all your needs according to the riches of His glory," but in James 1:22 (KJV), you are reminded you must be "doers of the word, and not hearers only." As you deal with this virus, remember not only to pray and ask God to keep you healthy and financially secure but also to practice good financial habits by being good stewards of what He has blessed you to have.

Unfortunately, you may be in a financial hole now, but I want you to know you can come out of the hole and become wise and successful in managing your finances in the future. Regardless of your financial situation, you can change it, provided you are willing to work on making the necessary adjustments. Too often, you fall in a financial hole and feel like you cannot get out of it, but if you set up a financial system and ask God for His guidance, it is possible to get out of your financial hole.

The first step to a better financial future is to stop believing the myth that you must get in debt to get ahead. Although many of you are financially literate, you have not applied the knowledge. Simply stated, you have some knowledge about what you should be doing, but you choose not to put it into practice. I want to offer some valuable recommendations to help you with a mental paradigm shift from how you have handled finances in the past to a new and improved way of managing your finances.

Debt Free

Most Fortune 500 presidents said that one of their main factors to being successful was not getting in debt. About the myth that many have about getting into debt to be successful is contrary to the truth. Typically, the less debt you have, the more likely your potential to becoming financially successful increases. Think about how you would have been able to deal with the coronavirus if you had no debt.

I heard various preachers say that we should be able to live off eighty percent of our total income. Leaving the remaining twenty percent, divided equally between tithes and savings. Take a moment and think about how much better financially prepared for a disaster you would have been if you had followed this practice since you have been in the workforce.

Unfortunately, most of you live off over 100% or more of your income. You charge things you want immediately with an attitude of as long as you can make the minimum payment your finances will be ok. I often say we live in a microwave environment, where we want everything right now and will pay for it much later. The problem with this ideology is we do not always look at how much we end up paying for things that we charge. It is unfortunate; many have forsaken the financial principles given to them by their parents. They did not have the opportunity to charge on credit because the charge card was not born until 1950. My dad told me at age eleven, when I had my first job as a paperboy, to save a nickel from every dollar I made. I wish I had listened to him. If I had, I would not have fallen in some of the financial holes that I have been through in my life. I would be in a better financial position than I am today.

Emergency Fund

Have an emergency fund for life events that eventually will happen. Everyone experiences things that occur outside their typical budget that can affect their cash flow. Things like car repairs, doctor bills, and home repairs are examples of things for which you should have an emergency fund in a separate account.

Budget

To manage your finances most effectively, everyone should have a budget, regardless of how much you make. I was teaching a financial class to inmates at the local county jail, and one of the inmates stated that he did not make enough to have a budget. I responded to him that having a budget would help to ensure that he is making the best use of what he makes. The less money you make, the less opportunity you have not to use it wisely. Identify other ways to prioritize how you are going to use what you make. No following your budget will have a more significant effect on meeting your most pressing needs, such as food, shelter, health care, and transportation.

Some people look at a budget as a restriction on how to spend their money. I like to rephrase it as a plan of how you will allocate what you make to meet your needs. The main problem that people make in using a budget is they fail to monitor how their actual spending habits track to their budget. If you see that you are spending more than planned, you either need to reduce spending in that area or reduce another budget category until you can find a way to increase your income.

Eliminating Debt

Earlier, I stated that the most effective way to improve your financial condition is getting out of debt. In the Bible, Proverbs 22:7, KJV states, "The rich ruleth over the poor, and the borrower is servant to the lender." Stated another way, when you are in debt, you are a slave to the lender. To change your financial position, you must stop the excessive charging and start living off what you make.

Next, set up a systematic plan to pay off your debt. You are paying off the smallest amount owed first by paying more than the minimum due each month. Once your lowest outstanding balance is eliminated, take the same amount, add it to the minimum payment of your next smallest outstanding balance. We call this the debt snowball. One mistake many people make is to pay off a debt, then feel they need to reward themselves. They take the money they had been paying on a bill and spend it on unnecessary items. You do not have extra money to spend on unnecessary items while you are still in debt! Stay disciplined and use the excess capital to pay off your remaining debt faster. Imagine how less stressful your life would have been if you were debt-free during this period of dealing with the coronavirus pandemic.

Savings for Major Loss of Income

I recommend that you set up a savings equal to at least six months of your monthly expenditures. Many suffer because they fail to plan for life challenges that may arise, like being laid off from work, having a major medical condition, or experiencing the death of a spouse who was bringing income to the household. If you find yourself in that position, you need to have a savings set up to help you until you can recover from the situation.

Retirement Savings

Investing in a retirement plan is a must. Set up a retirement plan so you will have the money to enjoy your retirement days. These plans can be a pre-tax plan such as a 401k, a 403b, or a 457 plan, which is the most basic plan offered for state and local government employees. These are ways to save for retirement. Many companies will offer a match on what you contribute up to a certain percentage of your salary. Plan to leave the funds in your account until at least age fifty-nine and a half, to prevent getting charged a ten percent early withdrawal penalty and having the total distribution added to your income for the current year. You can potentially end up in a higher tax bracket. Due to the coronavirus, most plans will allow you to take an early distribution.

A popular after-tax retirement plan is a Roth IRA. The biggest attraction for the Roth IRA is you are investing with funds that are already taxed. You will not be penalized or imposed with taxes on the distributions you take after age fifty-nine and a half. Therefore, the financial gain made on your investment is tax-free money.

Life Insurance

A good financial plan includes purchasing a life insurance policy. Many people have a misunderstanding about life insurance and look at it as burial insurance. They believe the only purpose of a life insurance policy is to pay for their funeral. A life insurance policy is to make sure your family can continue to live the lifestyle they were living before your death.

Before I go any further, I want to share some life insurance basics. First, any life insurance you have through your job is not owned by you; your employer owns it. If you leave the company, you will no longer have coverage and will have to get a policy based on your new age and health conditions. I always say that regardless of how much life insurance you have on your job, you should always have a policy you own.

The two basic types of life insurance are term and whole life. There are variations of each, but I am only going to discuss the two basic types. Term insurance is the first, and I would like to compare it to leasing a house. It costs less than buying it, but you have nothing to show for all that you paid into it. As long as you pay the agreed-upon amount per month, for the agreed-upon period, you have use of the house, and at the end of the lease, you have not accumulated any financial interest. Unfortunately, you then must sign a new lease agreement that will most likely be more per month either at your current residence or a new residence.

Term insurance works the same way. Whatever the term insurance policy period is, typically from five to thirty years, you are covered if you make your monthly payments. At the end of the policy period, you must get a new policy based on your new age and health condition. The new policy will cost more if you can even be covered. You may not be able to be covered if you have or have had certain existing health conditions.

The other type of life insurance I want to talk about is the whole-life insurance plan. I like to compare it to buying a house. If you pay the agreed-upon amount per month, you are covered; and, the policy remains the same regardless of your age and health condition. Whole life insurance costs more than term, but you build up a cash value that can be paid out to your designated beneficiaries on top of the face value of the policy if you were to die. You also have an option to borrow from the cash value and not affect the face value of the policy.

You should have a life insurance policy in place that will provide your family with enough money to bury you and continue living the lifestyle they were living while you were alive. To accomplish this, I recommend that you have enough life insurance to replace ten times your annual salary to pay off your mortgage and have enough money to pay for your children's college education.

As you may have already calculated, this could be a large number. I recommend getting as much whole life as you can afford and get the balance in term insurance. As you and your family age, the amount of life insurance needed will reduce because your home should be debt-free, and your children will be out of college. Based on this, you may have a term insurance policy for the amount to cover these items and not need to replace it when it expires.

I believe that everyone should have at least some whole life insurance. I lost a job in the mid-eighties. My wife was pregnant, and the only life insurance I had was through the job that I had just lost. I took out a whole life policy on myself and my wife. In January of 2009, my wife died unexpectedly, and the policy paid a death benefit to me. I kept the policy in force and early 2016, I went for my annual physical, and after the doctor received my EKG results, he stated I had to go to a cardiologist immediately to have a stress test done.

Shortly after, I had a double bypass heart surgery. The following month, my chest had to be opened again, due to an infection. A few months later, my heart was still weak, and I had to have a defibrillator/pacemaker inserted. Based on all I have been through, I would have a hard time getting life insurance now, if I could even afford it. By keeping the whole life policy, I took out in the mid-eighties, I know when I die, my family will have the money to continue living the lifestyle they are accustomed to living.

A spiritual or religious reason to have a life insurance policy is the Bible scripture (Proverbs 13:22, NKJV), "A good man leaves an inheritance to his children's children, but the wealth of the sinner is stored up for the righteous."

Wills

You must have a will and a living will. If you own anything, you need to have a will that designates who you want to receive your assets when you pass. You should have the will on file at your local courthouse. By having a will, you can specify who will receive your assets. If you do not have a will, your assets could be tied up in probate court until decided by the court, who is legally entitled to your assets. Probate court could be devastating to your loved ones as they will not be able to distribute your assets until the court decides. Also, this process could be quite expensive due to lawyer fees. Your estate will have to pay.

Also, I recommend you have a living will, so you can specify what medical procedures you may or may not want to have performed on you. You can also state whether you desired health care directives, such as being put on a respirator. By having both wills, you will help your family out both financially and emotionally.

Net Worth

Your Net Worth is the total value of all your possessions or assets, less everything that you owe or your liabilities. Everyone should know what your net worth is and strive to increase it. That number may be negative for some and positive for others. Simply stated, your assets minus your liabilities equals your net worth. I suggest that you calculate your net worth as soon as possible. Knowing your actual numbers will be your starting point toward financial freedom.

I also suggest that you stop unnecessary impulse spending! Eliminate the mindset of "just because I want it now syndrome." You will be amazed at how many millionaires you may have crossed paths with and did not even know it. The millionaire next door might be living next door to you!

Most millionaires do not show off by having flashy cars, overly stylish clothes, and super expensive jewelry. They dress conservatively, drive modest vehicles, and probably wear little jewelry. They developed the thought process and habit of investing their money wisely. They invest in things that appreciate rather than depreciate. Investing is what I want you to think about every time you get ready to spend your money on anything.

With every financial decision you make, ask yourself the following question. "Is this going to increase my net worth?"

If not, then ask, "Why am I buying it?" By asking yourself that simple, yet crucial first question, you should be able to change your thought process and spending habits. Developing this habit will eventually increase your net worth.

Summary

The principles, precepts, and processes discussed in this chapter provide a fundamental approach to obtaining and maintaining an excellent financial position. I do not expect everyone to do everything that I have presented. However, I hope everyone who reads the material will be compelled to evaluate how good of a steward they are in managing the income and blessing they receive.

For those who are thinking, I am already doing these things, I ask you to think of the words that my dad spoke to me years ago. "When someone is telling you something, even if you think you know everything they are going to say to you, listen; you just might hear something that you did not know. And if this is not the case, it does not hurt to hear it again."

I have quoted my dad various times in this chapter, and I thank him. He was a man with only an eighth-grade education, but he continued to teach me, a man with a college degree in accounting, on how to manage money until his death this past December. Thank you, Dad, for all the lessons you taught me!

—Calvin W. Denson, Sr.

CHAPTER 5

THE BUSINESS OF REAL ESTATE

By Harry Dock

My first writing experience came about when I was taking a fifty-minute bus ride to work. As the bus went through the different neighborhoods, it was a welcome sight to see the many ethnic groups and their culture. On this day, there was a young lady who was sitting in plain sight. I noticed she had a solemn look on her face. I sat there, trying to analyze what she could have on her mind. Two days later, my homeroom teacher announced that a local junior college was offering four scholarships to the students that could put together an English essay with a minimum of 1000 words. I wrote about the bus ride on the day that I tried to figure out what was on the young lady's mind. I titled it, "My World and Welcome to it."

About a month later, I was called to the counselor's office. I was the recipient of one of the four scholarships from the college. Now, came the more significant challenge. What was I going to major in? I was already working in the foodservice industry, so why not hospitality management and hotel, motel, restaurant management. I continued to work and educate myself in the food and service industry for thirty years, mainly in the Cleveland, Ohio area.

In 1989, I relocated to Chicago, taking on a position with the State of Illinois as a Food Service Sanitation and Safety Instructor with South Suburban and Moraine Valley Colleges. I also became a student test examiner with the state.

In the year 2000, I made a career change, and I became a mortgage loan officer. Within six months, I became one of the most productive loan officers. I won a four-day, all-expense-paid trip to New Orleans for my efforts. As I traveled through the mortgage industry, I became an office manager. I closed loans and supervised a staff of sixty people. I am currently working as a mortgage consultant, assisting homeowners, and soon to be homeowners with their financial needs.

In the early stages of my career as a loan officer, I worked for a mortgage banker with office locations throughout the United States. We handled onsite underwriting and processing at our one-stop-shop mortgage lending company. Once the underwriter (office manager) approved the file, it was passed on to the account executive to oversee the borrower signing all the necessary documents. During this process, titles and appraisals were used to validate the property value. We ensured that the title was clean, having no liens and that the borrower was the sole owner of the property. Once we completed the above, we scheduled the closing.

Most real estate transactions follow the same procedure. But keep in mind, a loan is not a loan until it closes. When refinancing a mortgage, the borrower has what is called the right of rescission set forth by the Truth-in-Lending Act (TLA). Under federal law, a borrower may cancel a home equity loan or line of credit with a new lender or cancel a refinance transaction done with another lender other than the current mortgage within three days of closing. So, in other words, all procedures which govern the process of refinancing must be fully exercised over three days. Once the loan is approved for funding, all funds are distributed according to the HUD (United States Department of Housing and Urban Development).

Most often, when refinancing your property, you have the option to pull equity out. The most common term is the cash-out refinance. Along with reducing your interest rate, in some cases, you can also lower monthly payments. You also may be able to reduce the length of the loan. If you have a thirty-year mortgage contract, you may be able to reduce your rate and term to a twenty, and in some cases, a fifteen-year term. The real benefit is the fact that a homeowner can save years of interest payments or thousands of dollars. A homeowner, providing that they qualify, can use their equity position to reposition their financial situation.

If you are seeking to increase your income through investing in real estate, using your equity position on your primary residence can give you the cash flow needed to build passive income through investing. Keep in mind that the banks treat investment properties as high-risk loans, and because of this, your Loan-to-Value (LTV) will be lower. Example: For the same property, if owner-occupied, the LTV could be eighty percent or better. But if non-owner occupied, the LTV could be ninety percent.

If you are considering real estate investing, you may consider purchasing multi-units. One unit may cover the mortgage and insurance, leaving the other units to provide an emergency maintenance building account. The remainder will be your positive cash flow stream.

Types of Mortgages

Conventional Mortgage: This is a thirty-year fixed-rate mortgage. Your monthly payments include property taxes, insurance, and monthly mortgage payments. A homeowner can set up their escrow account through the bank of their choice or pay the taxes and insurance on their due date.

Adjustable-Rate Mortgage (ARM): This is typically a thirty-year mortgage that adjusts in payments based on the terms and agreement on the Truth-in-Lending (TIL) statement. There are two types of ARMs. One is a 2/28; the other is a 3/27. After the two or three years are up, the index will determine the new interest rate. You must be aware of where the ceiling is. In other words, know the highest the interest rate can climb based on the index. One must be careful because once the interest rates adjust and reset higher, it could increase your payments. In some cases, this causes your property to become unaffordable.

Cash Purchase: For those of you who are seeking to pay cash for properties, you are in a good position because liquid money gives you negotiating power. Cash is king. However, there is much work to be done to protect the buyer and the seller—example—HUD!

Home Equity Line of Credit (HELOC): This is a type of loan where you are extended a line of credit based on the amount of equity that you have remaining in your home. You are only required to pay back the amount of the credit line plus interest. As long as you have not used any of the available credit lines, you are not required to make any payments. The HELOC is also known as a second mortgage.

Becoming A Homeowner

To become a homeowner, you must get a mortgage or pay cash. In order to become prequalified, it is essential to understand the need to do the following.

1. Reduce your debts and expenses.
2. Seek help cleaning up your credit.
3. Work on improving your credit score.
4. Cut down on spending and charging, especially on charge items that report to the credit bureaus.

Once you have accomplished the above-listed items, it is time to get preapproved. When you contact a loan officer, the below-mentioned information will need to be verified.

1. Application (1003)
2. Employment information
3. Income and assets
4. Proof of funds statement
5. Credit check
6. Down payment

Now, you are ready to meet with the real estate agent as well as a seller. Once you have found your home, the next steps begin. While you are working with the agent and seller, your lender and or mortgage broker and their team will compile the necessary documents for closing. The main report is the HUD-1, which distributes all funding in the transaction. Here is a list of the details addressed in the HUD-1.

1. Appraisal fees are paid outside of closing session
2. Title insurance fees
3. Attorney fees
4. Lender fee
5. Broker fees if an application is needed
6. Underwriter fees
7. Transfer stamp fees
8. Property inspection fees paid outside of closing
9. Homeowners insurance, which must be present at the closing
10. Real-estate taxes paid
11. Primary mortgage insurance
12. Accrued mortgage interest between the closing date and the first mortgage payment

Numbers one through twelve are the general outline of what home buying is all about.

Homeowners Assistance Program

Now that you are a homeowner maintaining your investment is the most important thing. However, there are unforeseen circumstances that arise. Health conditions may take a negative turn. Loss of a job or having a reduction in hours worked could impact your paycheck. You may be in an adjustable-rate mortgage (two years), and the index is rising, which means your payment may increase. Your Truth-in-Lending (TIL) Disclosure is an especially important statement.

It is advisable to seek the counsel of an attorney to be present at your closing to represent your interest. The current coronavirus pandemic has affected the financial climate around the world, causing a loss of jobs and unemployment rates to soar globally.

Homeowners with equity in your property, this may be an excellent time to pull cash out, depending on your financial situation. For those of you who have been impacted financially by the coronavirus, with little to no signs of financial relief in sight, this is the time to contact your mortgage lender to work out a program that will help you maintain your good standing with your lender.

Home Affordable Modification Program (HAMP)

The HAMP program is designed to assist homeowners who are in danger of losing their homes. Once you become thirty days late on your mortgage, you are in breach of contract, and you will be notified. If you become ninety days late, the loan will be escalated. During this period, the lender will give you options that can assist you in bringing the loan current.

Now HAMP program comes in to assist the homeowner. Often, they put the past due amount in the rear of the loan and lower the interest rate. This is designed to make your payments more affordable. Your lender will provide a list of options that can help you in getting your mortgage back on track. Keep in mind that it is only a loan modification. The most important thing is to communicate with your lender every week. The entire process usually takes up to ninety days.

Reverse Mortgage

A reverse mortgage is a select type of home loan that allows those who qualify to convert the equity in their home to cash.

If you are at least sixty-two years of age, your home is your primary residence, and you have equity in your home, you may qualify. As the homeowner, you are responsible for paying the property taxes, insurance, and maintenance. Keep in mind that the principal amount you borrow will accrue interest, and the original loan amount will grow exponentially. Upon your death, your heirs have up to one year to pay off the loan in full. I advise you to complete your due diligence to understand this process fully.

Home Sweet Home

In closing, becoming a property owner is one of the most significant investments that one could ever make. Keep in mind that property can be considered an asset or a liability. It can be perceived as an asset if you use it as a rental property. The renter will pay you monthly. In turn, you use the collected rent to pay the mortgage and other expenses. The renter helps you build up equity in your home while providing you with a stream of positive cash flow. OPM, also known as Other People's Money. A home can also be a liability if you live in the property. Add up all your monthly expenses associated with your home, and this is the amount of negative cash flow that comes out of your finances. Yes, you still build equity; however, you are also the funding source for this equity. It depends on how you look at things.

—Harry Dock

PART 3

PURPOSE, PASSION, POWER
FROM FEAR TO FEARLESS

CHAPTER 6

#HEALTHEHURT OR JUST REPEAT THE PAIN! WHAT YOU FOCUS ON EXXXPANDDS!

By Focus James

On Monday, March 9, 2020, right after school, I picked up my fourth grade, nine-year-old daughter, Simone, at the bus stop. She trotted behind me as usual. I was doing my early evening routine, preparing for my evening Zoom Life Coach and Public Speaking clients, and setting her up for her self-managing routine. She asked, with concern in her voice, "Mom, can I stay home tomorrow?" I asked, "Why?"

"Mommy, two parents, have been exposed to the corona, and I don't want to go to school. I'm afraid that I might get it."

I said, "Honey if that happened, they would have sent an email to inform us and make some provisions. NO tricking Mommy to stay home to have fun! You need to go to school tomorrow. However, if I hear something different by morning, I'll let you know."

To stay on schedule, I moved along. Ninety minutes later, the school district sent an email explaining that a local doctor was diagnosed, being treated, and quarantined due to the coronavirus. Others were also exposed. Some school districts were closed to clean the building and school buses. However, our school district would still be open on March 10, 2020.

I was in work mode and felt I needed to stay present with my clients and keep my child at peace. Later that night, when all of my clients were taken care of, and my fourth grader was fast asleep, I heard my late mother in my head saying, "You don't have to be anywhere you don't want to be. Let me know, and I will come to get you." At that moment, I was extremely concerned. Simone previously missed three days due to a fall at school that bruised her tailbone. I did not want her to lose any more school time. Yet, this was serious regarding the possibility of her getting sick and, more importantly, it was reported that infected children were not getting the full-blown symptoms of the coronavirus. They were bringing the virus home where parents and grandparents could contract the disease, so MY health was on the line. I decided I would sleep on it.

On Tuesday, March 10th, 2020, 7:06 AM, twenty-four minutes before it was time for Simone to wake up and get ready for school, I received an email. It was from two parents stating, (who happened to be married and working in our school district at separate schools), they were exposed to the local doctor, who earlier contracted the coronavirus. However, her school was still opening on March 10, 2020.

Extremely concerned, I texted a fellow parent, another friend that worked at a nearby school district, and a friend who was a vice-principal of a school in a neighboring state. The fellow parent has a master's in public health and was okay with sending her child to school because there was not enough data to warrant keeping her home. My friend, who worked at a nearby school district, confirmed that her district closed for deep cleaning, and she was not sure how soon they would reopen. My friend, the principal, suggested that I send Simone to school and reach out to the school district with my concerns.

Remembering Simone's scared little face and my mother's words of wisdom of self-care, I decided to keep her home and request her schoolwork to be sent home with my friend's child. Then the numbers for our county increased each day rapidly. I decided that Simone would stay home with me until further notice and that the school needed to send a homework packet. I requested that my child be excused, although it would be more than three days. Principal Rock responded with a call and stated, "Ms. James, I understand, and the days absent will be excused. We want to do what's best for everyone."

Note: As of April 24, 2020, a total of 3,294 confirmed cases of the coronavirus disease were reported in Montgomery County, PA.

For many people, dealing with the effects of the Coronavirus would have been a hardship. However, having my own business (as a Life Coach, Motivational Speaker, Public Speaker Trainer, and Business Coach) afforded me the privilege to continue functioning through Zoom meetings at home. My business picked up and eventually tripled in a matter of two weeks. Yes, it was difficult, but I was incredibly grateful for the new business.

I recognized how brave people were as they were self-quarantined in the house. No more overtime for me. No more girls' nights out. No more just staying out as long as possible, avoiding dealing with the pleasures, pains, and aches of relationships. People were messaging me constantly. Using my social media live streaming, engagements, and other events, people saw the need for my services. The birth of a new service began: "Create Your Virtual Business." I was so happy to be able to support people. My purpose and this historical moment had come face to face.

Two months earlier, I was seeking a backup plan for a supplemental source of income. I was doing okay in my business, yet not quite there. I applied for a substitute teacher position in my daughter's school district, amongst others. My stomach would churn as I thought that somehow, I did not put enough into my purpose during my one-year anniversary of being a full-time entrepreneur. I told myself, I could use it as an alternative to keep my ear to the ground and hear children and their plight and cause it to grow my business and myself. It is a good thing that I was choosing this type of supplemental income, but was it? Or was it that I did not use enough ingenuity to fulfill my purpose, and was I playing it safe to earn the $120 a day before taxes to secure my living? There were many questions I had to confront and ask myself. To find the answers, I reflected on times when I felt like giving up in the past but didn't.

Who did you become in the pandemic of COVID-19? When faced with hard times, we all get to see our growth or the lack thereof it. Case in point: At 18, I married a 21-year-old. We were Christians trying not to sin by not having sex outside of marriage. Thus, we produced 100 more problems by getting married out of season. We both loved God, but loving God is not enough. To create a sacred union and working institution, you need emotional intelligence, interpersonal skills, refined communication skills, and more importantly, you need to #healthehurt, or you will just repeat the pain! We both had not experienced life long enough, nor had we done the work to heal the pain from childhood and evolve.

Four years later, we were junior pastors, and his mom was the senior pastor. He left the house almost every day because of some church-related tasks. I asked to create a schedule and have family time. He insisted, "God comes first, and that's that."

I later found out he was cheating with our nanny, who doubled as my mother-in-law's armor-bearer. Ouch! I was not prepared for that revelation. I did not have the skills to deal with that level of betrayal, adultery, abuse, religious hypocrisy, and abandonment. His evil ways led to the foreclosure of our home, custody, and child support, and finally, a divorce.

I merely existed for the next ten years. My feelings were going in and out of some type of forgiveness. I never really healed from the hurt. I did not begin living my purpose until I was being picked up off my corporate job floor and rushed to the ER. I fainted because my manager had rescheduled the review of my evaluation for the third time. I was one of the best sales reps but did not receive a raise.

Going in and out of consciousness, I heard the EMTs discussing where to transport me. One EMT asked me my name, date of birth, and the date. She began to get aggressive when I could not answer. Then they began to talk about sports.

I was terrified as I heard the loud sirens and felt someone standing over me. They were asking me my name, and in the same breath, they began talking like we were not in an ambulance, and a sick person was not on their gurney. They were chatting as if they were on a park bench or waiting for a bus to come. I later reflected on that moment remembering my college guidance counselor's door arch, which stated: "Your Urgency is NOT my Emergency!" The stakes about what you are going through just may not be as high for others, as it is for you.

I awoke in the ER on a gurney. I saw my two-year-old daughter following behind my sixty-four-year-old mom in the distance down a hall of the hospital. I told myself, I moved on because I had a new long-term relationship that created a beautiful little girl. However, that moment sobered me. I could not speak, but tears started streaming down my face. The ER room is hushed in silence as it was the first time that I opened my eyes. My sister-in-law, a Pentecostal woman, whom I rarely saw get emotional, leaned while whispering, and asked, "Tanikia, what's wrong?" Slowly gazing away from watching my mom and daughter, I looked into my sister-in-law's tearful eyes and attempted to talk. I finally got it out. I said, "My heart is broken."

She leaned back, and a tear dropped from her eyes, streaming down her face. There was a gasp in the room, and people began to file out. It was a known fact that I was in a very tumultuous relationship with my daughter's father. I moved in and out of his apartment repeatedly before and after having our daughter.

Finally, I had the strength to go to "Women Against Abuse" for help. They graciously supported me through the process of getting a one-bedroom apartment and paid the first and last month rent and the security deposit. I was free! I was free from having to live with my mom and having to live with my daughter's father. However, my feelings stayed with me wherever I went! Imprinted in my mind that I was a victim, just like in my marriage and with this long-term toxic relationship, I created my job as the transgressor, the betrayer that was persecuting me.

Same Script Different Case
–Whitney Houston

During my recovery, I called my brother and asked, "Does your church still provide home Bible studies?" I was over with church. I had attended enough church for a few people, but I knew I needed to connect with God. He set it up. Mary, a happy and aesthetically pleasing woman, showed up. I was glad that she did not look homely and isolated from the world, which was my previous experience with church women. She began to go into the study.

However, my constant rebuttal of her explanation of the Bible and God led her to close the Bible and state, "You need Landmark!" I asked, "More than Jesus?" She replied, "You are so stuck you can't hear anything I am saying." She explained that Landmark Education would cause release and completion with my past and clear my present so that I can live in my future and its cost.

I told her it would take some effort to come up with the money but that I wanted to do it. She called a few people and was able to raise some funds towards the cost. I met with an introduction leader named Carol at Mary's house soon after and paid my down payment. The release and freedom of being stuck started on the drive there. By the time I left the introduction, I knew this was a turning point in my life. Completion was happening. A new conversation was born.

> A mind that is stretched by its new experience
> can never go back to its old dimension.
> –Oliver Wendall Home Jr.

On the first day of this three- and one-half-day course at Landmark Education, I forgave myself. I acknowledged that I had a choice to stay in all those relationships and subject myself to them. And now I could make a new choice because I was now conscious that I had the freedom to do so! I told myself I needed to stay at that corporate job because I had seven years in a four-week vacation, and I was going to break through the glass ceiling one day. I needed to stay because I needed to pay my rent and take care of my young daughter. Although I was miserable and there was some real injustice, I had to stay and take it because this was my plight. I told myself it was in my cards to suffer, given where I came from. However, I had a turning point, in Oprah's terms, it was an "AHA moment"!

Life is all choices. Choose it like ice cream: vanilla or chocolate.
–Landmark Education

My life was radically changed! I understood that my fight was still with my dad—his incapacity to be a father, his abuse of my mom, and his untimely death at my ripe age of ten. I got that he did the best he could with the information he had. I understood that my mom was a foster child who grew up in several different homes. She was the daughter of an alcoholic who also grew up in foster homes. She also did the best she could with the information she had.

I reconciled my struggle for forgiveness. I understood that my family members who molested me had their issues. I, too, needed to forgive them because all forgiveness is self-forgiveness. I forgave God for allowing me, at eighteen years old, to carry my ex-husband's and my first child for nine months, and then for her to die two weeks before delivery while still having a vaginal birth. I forgave God for allowing me to come to church, looking for healing. Instead, I was connected to a fundamentally unhealthy church that changed the trajectory of my life. I thought the notion of me getting married at seventeen was Godly. And so much more. As I was being released from my past, I began healing the hurt so I would not repeat the pain!

I continued the Landmark education while unpeeling layers of life with growth and with velocity. The Focus of Love concept was born through one of its courses. I had a vision of being a coach to help others heal. However, not yet being complete with my past, I knew it would be hypocritical. I knew it was my destiny and did not know how to get to it. Landmark became my bridge.

Then it happened! I called a former coworker from my corporate job to tell her all about Landmark Education. Before leaving the corporate world, she adamantly shared that the fantastic company she was going to would be perfect for me and that I should come on board.

I had no room in my mindset to even think about leaving the corporate world. She immediately jumped back into the conversation as if months had gone by, saying, "Focus, you would love this company. It is everything that you are. You get to talk with people about their problems and help them work through them. There is no rush, hurry, or time limit here. Unlike our previous company, we had a maximum of six minutes to communicate with a customer about what needed to happen. We tried to sell them something regardless of hearing that their spouse died, or their mom would be losing their home." It crushed my spirit to have to be that impersonal. I believed my different forms of depression were a result of me not being able to be human and be my expressive, extroverted self.

The lesson here is: "NO regrets of the past." We make the best choices with the information we have, and from the mindset, we are in during the moment of need. In the words of my late ninety-one-year-old G-Mom, "When you know better, you just do better."

How many of you are still in positions within your job or business, where it does not serve your soul, and it doesn't allow you to be your most authentic self? You have been doing the job so long or making such good money. You have ample vacation time or family ties, but you still allow yourself to suffer. I want you to know that you do not have to suffer in silence any longer. You can choose freedom! Choose to be your most authentic self! Test the power of freedom. What does it matter if your soul is not free? Peace of mind is often traded away for vacation time, a dollar, a bonus, and a "good life." How good is it if you suppress your unique design and purpose in this world?

I got my dream job! I talked to people and could be present with them. I connected with them in the most critical time of need. When they had cancer or delivering a baby, or when their child was going to rehab, I was their sounding board.

Then it happened again. Six years in, a new CEO changed the whole spectrum of how we did our jobs. I was devastated. Why did this happen? I thought I cleaned up my past. Why would I attract this type of energy again? Remembering what my life coach imparted in me, I concluded: "This is the way of the world. You may evolve, but it does not mean that corporate or any other entity around you will evolve. You have to be fluent and move like water." I concluded that it was time for me to move on.

The next gift I received was from my supervisor. She said, "Focus, you're no longer happy here, and I want you to go and do thefocusoflove.com full time. You're going to be wonderful, and you're going to do fine." She spoke purpose into my life.

I was worried. Could I do this full time? Could I be a relationship coach and a motivational speaker full time and sustain my family? I was stuck! I was afraid of failing again. Each time you go to the next level, you are reminded of your humanity or lack thereof. Moving on is an opportunity to evolve to be your most authentic self as you embrace the evolution of your soul on this earth. If you are NOT growing, then you are dying!

Fast forward, I did it! I ran with the opportunity, and now I serve thousands of people across this nation and in other countries. I get to speak life into people daily, transforming their inner souls, helping them to discover their purpose. My goal is to help you with getting the love you want and, in turn, the life you love. This journey all starts with the number one foundation, which is to #healthehurt, or you will just repeat the pain. It is not a question; it is a universal law. Newton's third law is, "For every action, there is an equal and opposite reaction." You must #healthehurt, or you will repeat the pain.

There is a price to pay to grow, and there is a price to pay to suffer, which price are you choosing to pay? Remember, NOT choosing is choosing by default.

Go to healthehurt.info for a FREE Training on Completing Your Past, or You will JUST Repeat the Pain. Email focus@focusjames. com, subject line: HEAL, and let's start your journey. Tell me what you need healing from and what your purpose is. If you do not know, we will discover it together.

—Focus James

CHAPTER 7

LEVEL UP!

By Constance B. Thompson

In 1981, I joined the United States Army Reserves. A year later, I transferred to the National Guard. Transferring was the best decision I made. My life was on a fast track. While serving as a guardsman, I got a job with United Cerebral Palsy as an Accounting Clerk. I was selected and offered the opportunity to enter a program called Active Guard Reserves (AGR). At the time, I did not know the payoff. All I knew was that I was living the life that I imagined when I was watching those soap operas.

With this opportunity, I was able to move out of my mom's house to Oak Park, Illinois, an affluent neighborhood in the west suburbs of Chicago. I say my mom's house because my dad passed in February of 1978 when I was fourteen years old. I served as an active guardsman for three years. Then I transferred back into the Army Reserves. While a reservist, I applied for a federal government job with the Department of Education and got it. I worked as an Equal Opportunity Specialist. The military promoted me simultaneously.

In 2003, I enrolled in the Sergeants Major Academy. While in the academy, I enrolled in Excelsior College and received my Bachelor of Arts degree. After I graduated from the Sergeant Majors Academy, I enrolled at National Lewis University. I received my master's degree in Human Resource Management and Development while still working for the federal government and serving in the United States Reserves.

Growing up as a child, my mom believed in natural remedies to cure illnesses. Her practices taught me a lot about herbal supplements. Today, I still use herbal supplements and teach my clients how to incorporate them into their lifestyle. When my mom got older, she was medically diagnosed with diabetes and heart disease. I believe her illness scared her because she turned from the naturopathic way of living and started relying on allopathic medicine.

I took a short break from the federal government to try to help my mom heal herself. I got into herbal books, attended workshops, and became a distributor for many multi-level marketing companies: Nature Sunshine, Melaleuca, and Pure Herb. I wanted to find out what was the root cause of my mom's disease. I learned all about the body's systems and how they worked. I went to colonic school and became a certified colon therapist. Out of all my studies, I knew that most problems started in the digestive system.

Shortly after receiving my certification, I opened a Colonic Center. Despite all my efforts, my mom passed in February of 2000. I continued to run my business until 9/11 hit. Then I had to close my center due to being deployed into active military duty. The military deployed me to several different places, including the Pentagon, for twelve years.

After active duty, I returned to my federal government job in Washington, DC. By law, my position was held for me while I served on active duty. I was treated as though I never left my old position. I still received all my benefits and incentives like everyone else. A year later, I retired from the military as a Sergeant Major. A year after that, I retired from the federal government. I served a total of thirty-two years.

During this entire time, I was still into my beautification: dressing well, wearing makeup, and thinking of ways I could make a difference in other people's lives. After my release from active duty, I immediately became a certified makeup artist and a Master Esthetician. And this is who I am! I want you to know that regardless of what route you take in life to become the person you want to be, there is always time to work on personal development.

Education

For personal development, the first thing you want to do is educate yourself in numerous ways. The traditional way is to go to school. If you do not have a high school diploma, you can go to a community college and take classes to obtain a general education development credential (GED). It is not a high school diploma, but it can get you into the military, or a university, and help you get a better job, more so than if you had no diploma or equivalent at all. If you are in high school, finish! Graduate! And go straight to a university and get the degrees of your choice. In this society, the more degrees, and certifications you have, the better chance you will have climbing the corporate ladder.

When I say go straight to a university, do it, because when you take breaks, they usually last much longer than intended. I took breaks, and it took me ten years to get my bachelor's degree. When I looked back, I realized that a lot of decisions I made delayed my success. When you choose to go to a university, stay enrolled until you graduate. Get a part-time job while you are in school to gain experience in your field so you could step into your career knowing you can request top dollar without much negotiation from the hiring team.

Maybe you are a person who says, "The hell with school, I am dropping out," or "When I am done with high school, that's it for me. I am going to become an entrepreneur!" If that's you, and you want to be a successful entrepreneur, you need to become a self-starter. Maybe a strategic planner, a go-getter, a salesperson, an accountant, and a marketer. Even an avid reader on subjects that are going to help you reach your goal. You will be all these things until you start making money to hire people to do them for you.

You are going to have to become laser-focused on where you want to take your business. You are the president of your company, and your business success or failure depends strictly on you. It is a good idea to go to seminars that you believe will help you with your business. You might consider investing in a coach. In the beginning, you will work long hours to kick-start your business off the ground.

There will be a lot of bumps in the road, a lot of resetting, and a lot of reinventing. Do not give up; stay the course. As an entrepreneur, you are teaching yourself how to become the best brand globally while staying two steps ahead of your competitors.

Regardless of what route you take in life, you will have to educate yourself. In life, there is no way around education. As a "program queen," education is still required. The government has plenty of programs you can choose from, e.g., housing, known as Section 8; food, known as the supplemental nutrition assistance program (SNAP); Special Supplemental Nutrition for women, infants, and children (WIC); and healthcare through the affordable care or Medicare. They even give you financial assistance known as supplemental security income (SSI). They help you pay your utility bills, but you still need to be educated on how to receive these benefits. The government has plenty of programs for those who qualify. So, how do you know if you are eligible? For the United States, call 800-318-2596 or visit usa.gov and educate yourself about the programs.

There is one last thing that still requires education. Besides traditional education and entrepreneurship, there are several people whose only purpose is to live off government services. In other words, this group of people has the blood-sucking leech mentally. Yes! I said leech mentality! These people use manipulation and conning skills. These types of people want everyone they know to support them. They are not interested in working a job or starting a business. They will ask momma, daddy, sister, brother, and anybody else for a dollar or two. We all know someone like this, and we even have them in our families. These people have learned how to master their skills. Their only purpose is to see who they can target to get whatever they can out of them.

The point I am trying to make in this section is education is a requirement! No matter what route you take in life, you will need to educate yourself.

Self-Awareness

What do you want in life? Where do you see yourself in the next year or two? Do you see yourself the same as you are now, or do you want to explode? If explode is your answer, then we need to find out your desires. I want you to sit down with a pen and paper and write down 100 things you would love to do or become in the next two years. Then, I want you to read it every morning and every night. Each night I want you to keep a journal and write ten things you are grateful for. Do this every night and watch how your life will start shifting to the things you have written on that paper.

Explore by visiting museums, art galleries, zoos, botanical gardens, symphonies, orchestras, and ballets. Learn ballroom dancing, an instrument, or a new language. Play tennis or golf; take a cooking class or become a gardener. All these things will shake your awareness and point you in the directions that you are trying to go. Remember to practice social distancing until the coronavirus has subsided!

Finances

I know this is a very touchy subject, but I must speak on it. We love to spend money on everything we do not need. My girlfriend and I used to go shopping together. I will be in the shops saying, "I know I don't need this," and her reply would be, "That's why we work—so we can buy the things we don't need." The crazy thing is I kept replaying that statement in my head, "I work, so I deserve to buy this and that."

At the checkout counter, the cashier asks customers to sign up for a credit card to save a certain percentage on their purchase.

Of course, at some point, I signed up for them to get more things I did not need. It was great because I could pay for it later and did not have to use cash. Taking this approach, I found myself buried in credit card debt. It took me years to dig myself out of that debt. I now say to myself, cash, and carry. If I do not have the money to pay for it, that means I cannot afford it. I now have one major credit card that I only use for emergencies and travel. I believed that just because I worked, I deserved to buy something. That was one of the most ridiculous things I could have ever said to myself.

Watch what you feed your mind. Watch the people you associate with and what they are feeding your mind. You can get caught up just like I did. Let me tell you, I was the sharpest, or shall I say, the most fly person you ever laid your eyes on. I was all into name brands—Hermes, Chanel, Louis Vuitton, Gucci, Burberry. You name it, and I had it. I was the cutest rich-looking person in my circle and probably the one with the least amount of money. Personal development is not about how expensive you look. It is about being smart about the choices you make in life and doing it with a lot of class (a subject I will get to later).

Here are seven helpful financial tips:

1. Stretch your money as far as it can go and build a nest egg along the way.
2. Whatever money you earn or require, always pay yourself first!
3. Save ten percent or whatever you can.
4. Put your savings in a different bank other than your primary bank.
5. Direct deposit your paycheck into your savings account.
6. Do not get an ATM card, and never touch your savings.
7. Take advantage of the company 401k retirement and Thrift Savings Plan (TSP). Most organizations match up to five percent.

Have you ever heard, "It's not about how much money you make; it's how much money you keep"? You work hard for your money. One day, you may want children, to buy a house, start your own company, or retire comfortably. These things all take money. Spending all your money to keep up with the herds or look fly is absurd! Be smart with your money. Live below your means and save. Remember, the sacrifices you make today will determine your future. Get into the habit of saving and investing.

If you need to educate yourself on money management, seek financial advisors like some of the authors of this book. We need to build assets and stop stacking up liabilities. If you do not know the difference, assets put money in your pocket, and liabilities take money out of your pocket. Start asking yourself the question: Is this item putting money in my pocket or taking money out of my pocket? Then decide what you are going to do. The decision is up to you. With every decision we make today, we determine our future. Remember that!

Self-Care

Caring for yourself should be your top priority. Women today have become lazy with their appearance. Their outfit of the day, every day, is stretch pants, a tee-shirt, or some sort of athletic wear. I see women in public carrying on like they had no proper upbringing and forgot how a classy lady should act. I've seen ladies in public talking loudly and cursing. Others were wearing too much make-up. Some were wearing pajamas and house shoes and tight-fitting clothes. Yes, some were wearing too loose-fitting clothes or too short of dresses with their breasts hanging out. The holey jeans, green, purple, blue, pink, or yellow hair, along with gigantic earrings and five rings on one hand, is a bit much. That speaks no class or desperation.

We are queens of the universe, and we should carry ourselves as such. The Bible states in Esther 1:17, "For this deed of the queen shall come abroad unto all women..." It also states in 1 Timothy 2, "that women adorn themselves in modest apparel..." Let's get it together, ladies! We can enhance our beauty by wearing little makeup, wearing clothes that fit and hair that matches our skin tone.

Just because a designer brings out some crazy trend, does not mean we have to run and buy it just to be in style. Stylish were the ladies in the fifties. Go back and look at how they dressed. I am not saying to pull out the white glove and the parasols. What I am saying is to look decent. Also, eat healthy, exercise, and take care of your teeth, hair, nails, and skin. If you need help with nutrition and skincare, I wrote a book titled *Forever Young,* and it sells on Amazon. I am also a personal development coach. Reach out to me for a free thirty-minute coaching session by calling 1-540-556-9158.

Mingling with High Society

To mix with this crowd, first, you would have to get the self-care part down. I live in an affluent neighborhood in Alpharetta, GA. I am a member of The Manor Golf and Country Club. It amazes me how people analyze a person who is new in this circle. Harvey Coleman's book, *Empowering Yourself,* hits the nail on the head when he speaks about moving up in leadership. He talks about how people in executive positions analyze a person physically and by communicating with them. They can tell what type of person you are by your appearance, how you interact, where you live, and what you drive.

The moving up in the leadership process amazes me. Whenever I meet a new person who lives in this country club community, they never fail to ask if I live in the country club community. Much of the time, when they find out that I do not, they quickly end the conversation and move on to the next person.

As Harvey Coleman explains, most people in this group start by watching how you dress (Country Club members are dressed casual or in golf or tennis attire) and how you care for yourself, e.g., your weight and personal grooming. They then ask you where you live, the different places you have visited, and how you spend your spare time. The Country Club crowd determines your level of acceptance by your income and other factors.

Are you the type of person that feels stuck and just wants to level up? Know that leveling up takes some work on your part. Work on yourself, learn how to network, and communicate with this group. Understand, leveling up has nothing to do with joining a country club unless that is what you want to do. Leveling up means surrounding yourself with the type of people you want to socialize with on a regular base. If it is the affluent group, you are going to have to make some changes from where you are today. Start with your appearance and mannerisms. Go to upscale restaurants, and more affluent nail and hair salons— purchase season tickets to sporting events and ballets. Start traveling to different places around the world and learning other cultures. If you want to mingle with high society, work on yourself so you can meet these people at their level.

Creativity

As I am writing this chapter, we are in the worst pandemic I have seen in my lifetime, the coronavirus! This deadly disease has isolated the nation and killed many people. During this stay-at-home, order/isolation is not the time to feel scared or get depressed. Now is the time to show the world who you are and what you can do. Instead of sitting around binge-watching all your favorite shows on Netflix, or wasting time watching all the sad news on television, get creative. You know the online business you wanted to start that the cakes you bake are amazing, and everyone you've shared them with tells you they are delicious, and they need to be on the supermarket shelves. What about that instrument you wanted to learn how to play, and you just did not have time to indulge because you were just too busy or tired? You now have all the time in the world for a new you.

Do not let the coronavirus or negative news put you in a position just to sit and waddle in negativity and fear. Get up and enhance what you already have going on or create something new. Make masks. Start your hand sanitizer line. Create your disinfectant wipes since these are the items people cannot find in the stores. If you are a teacher or have a skill you want to share with someone, start a Udemy class on Udemy.com. Sit back and ask yourself, "What have I always wanted to do and just could not find the time to do it?" Do it now!

Closing

I hope you were encouraged by reading my chapter on personal development. I intend to transform your thinking about where you are now and what you want to be in the future. You are the captain of your ship, and no one can direct it like you. I challenge you to do something different, that will move your life forward. To be the queen, you are and to always remember, the decisions you make today will determine your future.

—Constance Thompson

CHAPTER 8

S.M.A.R.T. – AUTHENTIC JOURNEY

By Beverly Hammond

*The graveyard is the richest place on earth because it is here
that you will find all the hopes and dreams
that were never fulfilled.*
—Les Brown

During the first week of March 2020, a colleague posted a disturbing video to a social media platform I monitor. In the video, Asian people are going about their daily routine until an adult male collapsed onto the sidewalk. My colleague's caption read, "They are not telling us everything."

I was scheduled to participate in a workshop in the Houston area on Saturday of the same week. On Friday, the host of the event sent me a text, postponing the event due to public safety concerns. These sudden turns of events seemed strange at the time. I had no idea they were related and were indicators of an imminent condition that would alter normal as the world knew it.

As I pen this chapter, the world has come to a halt due to the COVID-19 pandemic. Many people have weighed in on the global challenges resulting from these circumstances. I have experienced greater personal introspection.

Some time ago, I came across a video titled, *Are you a connector?* The premise was quite interesting. The narrator pointed out that we continue to be educated within an industrial assembly line paradigm, although the world is moving toward an age of innovation and collaboration.

We are no longer content on being forty-year cogs in an economic wheel that keeps turning to suit its purpose. I believe this pandemic, despite the tremendous challenges it has produced, will also usher in an era of individuals who are more committed to achieving personal goals and fulfillment. I believe that many will have the courage to use this global timeout to reset their lives and will need a process to help navigate their journey of fulfillment and purpose.

The Wrong Question

I started my journey of purpose in 2015 after more than fifty years of living within a belief system that began for me as a little Black girl reared in a Southern Baptist culture from a small town in Mississippi.

Throughout my formative years, adults asked me, "What do you want to do when you grow up?" Because I excelled academically, my family had high expectations for my success. I assumed I would use those talents to make it happen. I thought that what I would do professionally would determine who I became. My profession would define me, and my success would fulfill me. I did complete a twenty-year military career. I built a twenty-year business and realized I had what most would consider a successful life. That was until my belief system started to unravel, and I had to ask myself some difficult questions.

A friend introduced me to books, concepts, and content that I had never been exposed too. Not socially, financially, metaphysically, or historically. The more he shared, the more I became thirsty for knowledge. A whole new world began to open for me. I was hungry for more. The more I read, the less the world I thought I knew was a fit for me.

In July of 2016, the trajectory of my life would shift forever. One morning, I found myself in a YouTube rabbit hole, bouncing from one video to the next. I came across a video of the police shooting of a thirty-two-year-old Minnesota black man, Philando Castille. This incident was one of many unjustified police shootings of Black men during this window of time. I did not know this young man in any personal way. But I found myself weeping as I looked on. For days, I was overcome with emotions, ranging from grief and anger. A feeling of urgency and activism came alive. This event felt like the fire that lit the fuse on a stick of dynamite and exploded inside of me.

The explosion inside of me was my belief system imploding, making room for an empowering belief system that would fuel this new path. From this experience, I realized I had never thought to ask myself, "Who do I want to become?"

Five years later, with a lot of trial and error, I can articulate a process that emerged to help me be more effective on my journey of purpose, fulfillment, and pursuit. Now, I know who I am becoming in this world because of how I show up every day.

S.M.A.R.T is the Journey

Before I share, I must make a disclaimer. My husband says I have an obsession with turning every concept into an acronym or mnemonic. I am guilty as charged, and you are now warned.

At the beginning of this chapter, I shared a quote by Les Brown, one of the most prolific motivational speakers in the industry today. To his point, many people fail to live a fulfilling, self-actualized life that inspires fantastic ideas and creativity. The desire to have a fulfilling life is just the beginning. To have an effective process to get it done is the key. Unfortunately, this process is not taught by traditional institutions.

In the first five years of my transformation, I made many mistakes. I had zeal, but my talents and skills were in information technology. The habits that served me well in my initial successes impeded my ability to grow into this person I was becoming. Additionally, I was exhausting my financial resources doing all the wrong things.

Although the past five years included some of the most painful experiences of my life, a process emerged that I am using to help others transform their lives from cog to purpose. It is the S.M.A.R.T. process, a mnemonic for Spiritual awareness, Mental capacity, Action-centered, Resource intelligence, and Team integration. The five S.M.A.R.T. pillars present a holistic context for taking control of how you show up in the world.

As I present each pillar, I will use the metaphor of a vehicle to highlight the significance of developing each area for leveraging the success of your purpose-driven journey. I challenged myself to create a practical approach to present the five pillars within the context of this chapter. Then it occurred to add dimension to these concepts by providing companion videos filled with activities to help you, the reader, build your S.M.A.R.T. process. As you read each of the pillars, I invite you to jump over to my YouTube channel, *SMARThentic,* to check out the related videos.

Spiritual Awareness: The Steering Device

It is true that if you want different results, you must do things differently. My journey of purpose has been a composite of teachable moments. A lot of time and resources were spent in the pursuit of "shiny objects" –those opportunities that made sense on the surface but were simply distractions. I could not make that distinction at the time because I did not have a clear purpose. I believe the underlying challenge most people face in pursuit of their greatness, as referenced to in the opening quote, is finding clarity, focus, and the ability to execute. Knowing your purpose is the necessary linchpin.

The word purpose is tossed around a lot in today's vernacular. As we are developing a more enlightened world view, we have become more fixated on personal empowerment and meaning. Eventually, I began to focus on purpose. But I was stumped. The words' purpose, mission, and vision were used a lot and often interchangeably. As I have matured in my journey, these three words reflect a progression in action and results. But I must also add passion and principles to the list.

While succeeding in realizing your life purpose, your authenticity is imperative. Our spiritual awareness is the most genuine connection to our authentic self. As one philosopher puts it, we are spiritual beings, having human experiences. The spirit within us drives our desires to be and do. These desires manifest as passions that dominate our thoughts, decisions, and actions.

Our thoughts are fed through the filters of our belief system to determine which set of rules we should follow. These rules, whether consciously or subconsciously, are the guiding principles for our decisions and actions.

Once I understood the relationship of passion, purpose, mission, vision, and principles, I had a context that indeed gave me clarity and focus. Then I began executing. I offer the following sequence of activities to start your purpose journey:

1. Identify YOUR PASSIONS by searching for the burning desires within. You will know when you find it because it will start to dominate your thoughts.
2. Define YOUR PURPOSE by asking how your passion can empower and enrich the lives of others.
3. Create YOUR MISSION, which is the plan of action to realize your purpose.
4. Determine YOUR VISION, by setting goals which demonstrate that you are carrying out your mission and realizing your purpose.
5. Practice YOUR PRINCIPLES to remain authentically you.

Mental Capacity: The Engine

Once you have defined your purpose, mission, and vision, you can begin steering your life in the desired direction. But just as a vehicle relies on its engine for power, you too must have a powerful engine to complete your journey of purpose. Your mental capacity is the engine of purpose. Your journey of purpose will be unchartered territory for you. Up to this point, you have been a cog in someone else's engine.

You will be in the driver's seat, and there are many mental skills you must develop. I have narrowed them down to four characteristics: courage, optimism, determination, and elasticity. These characteristics have become my mental C.O.D.E.

Starting with courage, this is your "get out of jail" card. Your journey of purpose will demand new beliefs and new norms. Once you have decided to start this journey, you will encounter resistance from every direction, especially from the people that are the closest to you. You will need the courage to break out of the prison of their expectations of you. You should start by using this mental code to break out of the prison of the limiting expectations you have placed on yourself.

Peeling this onion will be difficult and discouraging. You will have to feed yourself heavy dosages of optimism and faith continuously. Affirmations and empowering statements must become part of your daily ritual.

Then you must become determined to keep it moving through the good and bad times. Many things will not go as planned. There will be lots of lessons to learn from. For each setback, the reaction must be to assess the situation, make the necessary adjustments, and get back into your journey.

Lastly, elasticity is critical. If you are in a new space of living with purpose, you don't know what you don't know. You must be open to new things. You must be willing to evaluate information, encounter new experiences, and when appropriate, and adopt them into your journey of purpose.

Action-Centered: The Wheels

The third pillar of the purpose vehicle is action centered. It is the wheel because action drives the realization of the vision. This pillar seems like the easiest one. However, it is the most elusive in a society where success is defined by production. We have become busy people. The work ethic that contributes to your life success before your purpose journey will be significant.

However, I eventually discovered that being busy did not mean that I was progressing toward realizing my vision. It turned out that I was just exhausting myself. And, in many cases, depleting valuable resources.

Over the last few decades, the phrase time management has become synonymous with productivity. But there is a distinction that is seldom made. You must focus on doing the right things to effectively overdoing things the right way to be efficient. Being effective produces impact. Being efficient creates an effect with few resources. In your journey of purpose, the impact must come first. Therefore, I propose a structure that achieves time balance through activity management. This structure is explained in detail on my YouTube channel, *SMARThentic*.

1. You must determine the ROLES of your life, including the role(s) added by your journey of purpose. We are individuals, spouses, parents, professionals, and friends. Each of these roles has different needs and requires our attention.
2. Once you have outlined your roles, make a list of the related responsibilities. I created a responsibility triangle, putting the most significant responsibility on the bottom tier.
3. One of the biggest reasons we fail to accomplish our goals is because we tend to give lots of time to the tasks we enjoy doing and little or no time to the jobs we dread doing. To avoid this imbalance, every responsibility within each role must be given scheduled time. This process is known as time blocking. For a given week, ensure that you have scheduled time for each area of responsibility.

4. To evolve beyond doing only the fun tasks, prioritize tasks based on significance. In his book *7 Habits of Highly Effective People*, Stephen Covey made a distinction between urgent and important tasks. Critical tasks are time-sensitive tasks, usually brought on by procrastination or unforeseen circumstances. Important tasks are tasks that are necessary to achieve success, generally demanding consistent attention. Each responsibility has both urgent and essential tasks.

5. Lastly, monitoring task completion can be simplified using an automated tool. There are many tools in the marketplace. I suggest using a tool that allows you to document your roles, classify your responsibilities, and schedule your important and urgent tasks.

Resource Mastery: The Fuel

One definition of resource states, "A source or supply from which a benefit is produced and has some utility" is fitting for your purpose journey. You must-have resources, especially financial resources. You must begin by developing and implementing a passive income financial strategy to secure the resources needed to maintain a standard of living. Then you have time and freedom to pursue your purpose.

We are programmed from the cradle to get an education, get a good job, buy beautiful things, work for forty years, and then retire. If you work forty to sixty-hour weeks for forty years to support your family, when will you have time to pursue your purpose?

That was my epiphany. As a self-employed database engineer for almost twenty years, I realized tremendous financial success. But I worked fifty-plus hours weekly. One day, as though a switch suddenly flipped, I did not want to do that anymore. During the time Philando Castille was killed, my activism within the narrative of the challenges of Black America was a priority, and my purpose was alive.

However, earning an income by trading my time for dollars was the only process I knew. It took financial experts, such as Robert Kiyosaki, to introduce me to the concept of passive income. I became obsessed with the principle of passive income, generating income without the constant demand of my time. I started participating in workshops, seminars, and mastermind programs to learn how to develop the right strategy. The right strategy would eventually provide the resources to build the standard of living I desired. It would give me time freedom to devote to my purpose and provide some capital in support of my mission.

I felt obligated to invest in my financial knowledge. Knowledge reveals more options for financial security and time freedom. I eventually launched Black Wealth Consortium, a platform that promotes these principles.

Team Integration: The Passengers

Thus far, the focus has been on your journey. But your purpose will involve people. People that inspire you. People that mentor or coach you. People that serve you and people whom you will serve.

It is crucial to understand which position the people in your life occupy. Building relationships is the most challenging element of your journey. Relationships often originate and evolve without the proper frame of reference, and everyone is viewed from a single prism. That approach is the easiest but typically leads to challenges and misunderstandings. If you take the time to figure out the roles of the people in your life, you can define your behavior and your expectations of them from a perspective of clarity.

People who inspire you tend to connect at the soul level. You probably will want to emulate them in some way. People who mentor or coach can motivate you and assist in your transformation. These people represent authority, so leverage the value they bring to your life.

People who serve you bring skills and talents to get the job done. Be clear as to what you need from them and have objective forms of measurement and accountability. Emotions have no place here.

Lastly, your purpose journey will be measured by how you empower others with your service. It is essential to understand the impact of helping others to start and complete their journeys.

Time to Start Your Journey

Your journey of purpose will have many twists and turns. Having a process to fall back on will minimize the cost of your time, as well as mental and financial resources. The S.M.A.R.T process reflects the lessons I have learned along my journey. But I am just finding my lane. There is much more to do. So, I welcome you to start your journey. Let my lessons become your teacher by checking out the companion videos on my YouTube channel, *SMARThentic*.

—Bev Hammond

CHAPTER 9

POETRY – THE BUSINESS OF SPOKEN WORD

By Wanisha Johnson

Before heading home, the agent was making her last stop of the day, which was at her office. Walking in the door, she saw her secretary, Sam, smiling as she always did. Racing to grab the stack of sticky notes on her desk, Sam began to tell her all the messages she had written on them. Explaining there was one client that received the documents he needed to move forward, Sam informed her that the client wanted a five-bedroom house, and he also wanted to start looking tomorrow. She thought it seemed like an unreasonable request because it was just him and his wife. Maybe they want a family, she thought.

She spent hours searching and creating a list. The initial search yielded 126 properties. The agent sifted through the list, making sure she had met her client's needs. Checking for all the major and minor details, she picked the absolute best and closest to perfect homes. Knowing her clients would be ecstatic about the options she had chosen, she told them which address to meet her at first. They arrived thirty minutes early.

Upon crossing the threshold, they felt their dreams coming true. The very first questions they asked were, "How many bedrooms does it have, and what's the asking price?" Her answers erased all the joy that previously warmed their hearts. They responded that they informed Sam that they wanted a five-room house, not a five-bedroom house. It took an exceptionally long time for those clients to see anything else they liked. But eventually, they did.

Valuable information can be gained or lost with excellent or poor communication. While we spend a lot of time communicating with those around us, we must not forget to talk with ourselves as well. We are ever evolving. Accepting our imperfections, while being as magnificent as we are, we are always striving to be better.

Matching a client with a home that is in their budget, that they cannot wait to call their own, is a gratifying feeling. It can be a lengthy process or smooth sailing. Either way, it is utterly worth it in the end. Although I am joyful in my career, as with most professionals, it can be rather demanding. There are people to meet, appointments to make, inspections to conduct, repairs to schedule, and calls. Then more calls. And more calls. There is a lot of talking, but also a lot of listening, which is essential in the communication process.

A few years ago, I was speaking to a potential client about normal activities associated with the buying process. Preapprovals, search criteria, maximum purchase prices, basements, garages, and the number of bathrooms, amongst other things, were discussed. To my surprise, we became acquainted rather quickly. That could be because a mutual friend referred him. The conversation progressed into him, picking out a few homes he wanted to view. That, in turn, led to availability concerns. But we professionals know how to work around that. We just call everybody back and change the time if possible. We will change the appointment day if necessary. The "show(ing)" must go on.

We were on a more open level at this point. My friend proceeded to explain that the reason he could not make the property showing was because he was performing. That could mean many things. I had no idea what he meant, and I must have shown confusion on my face. With laughter, he acknowledged my confusion and told me he was into the arts, mainly poetry, and spoken word.

He was excited to show me the flyer, but his phone's battery was low. The screen had gone dark. So, like a good neighbor, I let him use mine to look it up. He told me the names of people who were expected to be there, and he was utterly excited. It sounded exciting to me too! He also told me there would be an open mic. That is when people not expected to be there, come to the event, and want to perform. He asked if there was something that I would be interested in doing or attending? I told him that I used to write but had never been on stage. The big lights, the quiet scene, the audience—all makes me want to run in the opposite direction!

I went on to say that, even though I did not want to get on stage, that did not stop me from wanting to go. He called me a chicken, and we made plans to meet up later after we both made it home and freshened up. When I arrived at the event, he had already gone in. He went to put his jacket on a chair at a table, just to make sure we would have seats.

The scenery was relaxed and energized at the same time. I did not know what to expect, but I was there for it all. There were all kinds of talented people there. I had a great time. It felt like I was in my element. Being there inspired me to want to go home and find my old notebooks. We were so wrapped up in experiencing the art that we almost ended the night not agreeing on a specific time for the property showing scheduled for the next day.

Out of nowhere, the doorbell rang. It was maintenance. To my surprise, maintenance came to do the repairs we scheduled, that slipped my mind. There I was, it was Friday, and I had a long week! Contractors were walking back and forth, using loud power tools, working, and I had enough. I picked up my notebook and began to thumb through the pages. Forgetting and remembering all the times my pen communicated with the paper. It said all the things I could not. Or would not. With no previous plans and nowhere in particular to go, I decided on going to open mic, night, it was. I took my notebook with me just in case I got over my stage fright and decided to recite something. I parked outside the venue and started flipping thru the pages trying to decide which one I should do.

"She is a diamond in the rough, just waiting on somebody to find her." No, that one's too gender-specific.

"When you're feeling like defeat has had too long a last and happiness is now a part of your past when your faith is still strong but seems like it isn't gonna last, hold on." No, that one is too heavy.

"I've dreamt of the day that my fears would fade away, and that special one would come along to fill that empty space." No, too needy.

"If I stop and think and look, but don't blink." No, too.

As time drifted away, I convinced myself more and more that I needed different materials to present. I also noticed I was missing the show. That night, I did not decide to read.

As soon as I walked in the door, I felt like I was able to exhale. No one knew me. It was the energy and good vibrations in the room. There was nothing wrong with my first experience, but this was much different. I still cannot quite explain it, but I am glad I went. I am grateful for all the connections and conversations that led me there. It felt like home. What started by communicating with a client, ended up reintroducing me to my center—writing and speaking.

There is always something to communicate. Needs, wants, hopes, dreams, business, love, etc. All can be conveyed through communication. It is a skill that can make a difference in your personal and business life. Keep in mind that there is a difference between communication and effective communication. Anyone can technically say anything they want. That does not mean it will come across as intended. Things should be presented in different ways in different situations to different people.

There are four types of communication: verbal, nonverbal, written, and visual. As we all know, the primary method of expressing oneself is through verbal communication. In a professional working environment, excellent verbal communication is a must. It can make you stand out as a job candidate seen as confident and knowledgeable. There are meetings and conferences held that require adequate communication skills. Whether as a team or just one person, duties and responsibilities must clearly be explained and acknowledged. If either party is a poor communicator, there will be mishaps in the job performance and or friction between individuals.

On a more personal level, excellent verbal communication is a must. Although sometimes there is nothing you can say to get through. Then again, sometimes there is. Listening is a part of being able to communicate effectively, and it is essential in being successful.

A strong communicator knows that at some point, they must connect with their audience. If you are not connecting, you are just talking. Most times, when we communicate verbally, the words are said with a desire to be digested and understood. Granted, people may hear you but are they listening, and do they understand what you are saying, is the question. Along with getting your point across, you must listen to effectively communicate.

I began going to those poetry sets often; it became a planned event for me. I would recite my pieces at home alone and in front of friends to prepare myself for when I got on stage. I knew that day would come. There was so much love, acceptance, encouragement, and strength in the room, that there was no other place I even considered reading. About the fifth time I went, I walked in the door, and the lady gave me a big hug. She then said what she always said. She told me who the feature was and asked, "Do you want to sign the list?" That day, I said yes.

As you walk through new doors, you will find new challenges that greet you. Do not allow problems to hinder your progress but to sharpen your sword.

As I took my seat in the audience, I immediately thought, "I need a drink." It was that kind of nervousness settling in. I started doing all the anxiety relief exercises I had been researching in hopes of counteracting the stage fright. I was concentrating on my breathing and saying affirmations. I guess this is the moment I picked to start effectively communicating with myself. The bottom line was—do it anyway. I had to permit myself to stumble because nobody's perfect and permission to be great because I was born that way.

My nervousness did not go away. Every time the MC was about to call an artist up, my nervousness would go back up, out, and through the roof. It would taper down, and then climb right back go up like a rollercoaster. I had never felt like that before, but I did not leave because I told myself to do it anyway.

Sometimes, communication needs to be with yourself.

That was about seventeen years ago, and on that night, I heard for the first time, "Put your hands together for our next performer. Coming to the stage is Logic." And just like that, it was showtime. I tried to swallow the lump in my throat to no avail. There I was, on stage, behind the mic, with the silence and the lights. It was almost surreal up there. I took one deep breath, and I began

"My pen redirects thoughts to paper.
No pencils.
Remove the eraser.
Because mistakes are meant to be made.
I'm out here trying to change the world.
I don't need the credit.
It could be behind the scenes moving black card money.
Like, I don't need the credit.
This world can make you believe it's hard to succeed.
But, only if you let it.
And never be guilty of not following your dreams.
'Cuz trust me, you'll live to regret it.
You can't expect respect if you're not respectful.

To give it, is the only way to get it.
If you put in work, eventually things will work.
Still, you get what you give.
Reach for the sky.
Believe you can fly.
But also watch out for planes.
If you properly prepare, there'll be less wear and tear.
Though every pilot must earn their wings."

—LogicNMotion

My heart was pounding; my mind was racing; the applause, I could not hear. My thoughts were racing at full speed. I calmly stepped off the stage, walked down the aisle, and straight out the door. My heartfelt like it was beating out of my chest. That was exhilarating and terrifying at the same time. Eventually, I became comfortable enough to stay after my performances. After some time, I started talking in depth to the other people there. I found that the world is small, and love is big. I would have never known how connected we all were, had I not stayed around. Connecting with everyone would not have happened if I did not take the time to communicate with them. I followed that venue for about ten years—the people, the events, everything—until the host moved out of state.

All these experiences and life-changing moments happened because I took the time to communicate with a client. We looked up a flyer that prompted more events of the same likeness. That was social media communication. It is incredible how one step always leads to another. That was Divine Order communicating with me. There are times when you must get on their level.

The level of communication used in speaking at a business meeting, on stage in front of a group of people, to a cashier about an overpriced item, or any other situation, would not be the level of communication you would use while speaking to a two-year-old child. Considering your audience when communicating is essential. You can explain something to all those people, in one way, but there is no guarantee they all will understand it that way. The goal is communicating in such a way that they can individually understand. Then you will have effectively communicated.

My writing has evolved by leaps and bounds over time. I now share without reservation, the gift that gives me purpose.

As we journey on, there is always something to improve. There are new phases to explore. There are new levels to reach. It is a never-ending task with all kinds of challenges in the middle. Be fully aware that things can get uncomfortable when you are growing. You are going to stretch out of some places because you are growing. You may have to be verbal and vulnerable in areas you chose not to visit in the past. And that is ok. The magic is in the next steps you take.

Every day presents us with another chance to be successful. With determination and action, you can accomplish anything. If there is a passion you have, then explore it. If there is a career you want, apply for it. If there is a hobby you love, indulge in it. If there is a dream you have, then live it!

—Wanisha Johnson, LogicNMotion

PART 4

The Non-Profit World
It's Better To Give
Than To Receive
(Acts 20:35 KJV)

CHAPTER 10

THE MISSION FOR SISTAH'S HOUSE
GOD, WHAT'S NEXT?

By Crystal J. Crockett

*The thing that most consistently controls our success or
failure is our actions. What we do or don't do impacts
our ability to experience the success we're seeking.*
—Rev. Dr. Derrick B Wells

I discovered this truth while looking backward: I wish I could say that I was diligent in my pursuit of being a business owner, but that is not the case. My business, Sistah's House of New Beginnings, was conceived in 2014 but was birthed in 2018, several years later. Looking back, I can now see how each step – though seemingly out of place – had a definite purpose for being there. Like the bricks paving the railroad along 95th Street in Chicago, what seemed mismatched and out of place was a necessary piece to the final product.

I received the idea for Sistah's House from my Higher Power during a time of serious prayer. Working as a special education teacher with youth was a role I enjoyed, but I eventually lost that position. As a person of faith, I went on a quest of prayer to find out my next steps. I received the idea to help young women, which was something I enjoyed but found limiting in my role as a special education teacher. In passing, I mentioned the idea of starting a nonprofit for young women to my support system: my sister, my niece, and my best friend. Each of us had experience working with children in different capacities. Perhaps this collective experience was one of the things that bonded us all together.

Receiving their unanimous approval was the next step along the path. Although we did not have a name for the nonprofit, or even a full picture of how it would operate, we knew there was a need for it in Chicago. And we felt we could make it happen. The board of directors had taken shape, and I was pushed to the forefront.

Being a special education teacher, I noticed my students gravitated to me, especially the young girls. Now, I am a mother of boys, I have a bonus son – he is my stepson, but I don't call him my stepson, I call him my child – and I have a son that I birthed. Thus, I was not accustomed to working with young girls, but I noticed as I was teaching that the young girls gravitated to me. Although I am firm with my instruction and how I conduct my classroom, I express love and genuine concern for my students. Perhaps, this is why young women always wanted to talk with me about various issues they were experiencing. I found it was pretty hard for me to have time for myself when I was in the building because if I was in my office – I was a case manager as well – at least three times per week I was approached by young women who wanted to talk to me about an issue they were experiencing.

Receiving my bachelor's degree in business and project management were helpful but did not adequately prepare me for starting a business. There was so much to consider. The challenge became daunting. I learned that Loyola University's Law Department offered pro bono services, and I was able to connect with them for my next steps. Their guidance was invaluable! They walked us through the process and helped us complete all the checks and balances suggested for starting a nonprofit. Thanks to them, the documentation was done. The building blocks, the foundation was now laid. And once again, I waited.

I sat on it because I did not believe it was something I should do. I kept having all these excuses as to why I should do it. I felt uncomfortable. I felt uneasy. I knew I was not living my best life, but I just could not figure out what steps I needed to take next. "God, what's next?" I kept asking.

I am so fortunate that my son and I have such a great relationship, even though the expression of our faith is quite different. Sometimes he will attend church with me, but his life path is different than mine, and I respect my son enough to give him space to live his own life. So, imagine my surprise when he said to me, "You're not doing what God has for you, and until you do, Mom, you're going to continue to spin your wheels."

Out of the mouths of babes, right? I needed to seek spiritual counsel after this revelation.

During a long, in-depth conversation, I shared my vision for Sistah's House with my pastor for whom I have the utmost respect. With as much detail as I could at the time – which wasn't much – I spoke about my desire and my fears, knowing that my pastor, who was also a savvy businessman, would give me honest, sober counsel. I braced myself for his response. In his deliberate, eye-to-eye communicative style, he said that he could see the manifestation of the vision, that he could see me doing it, and go and make it happen.

Me: "Go and make it happen?"

Pastor: "Yes, go, and make it happen!"

I received more sage words of wisdom before leaving his office. My Pastor instructed me to continue my prayer work so that God Himself could elevate me to be the person I needed to be, for the vision to manifest. Hmm. More work to do. Not only did I have to go and learn how to start a business, but now I had to work on building my faith, strengthening my beliefs, and recreating myself.

I came back to my team and told them that I was ready to move forward with the nonprofit. I did not realize that my team was waiting for me. From that point forward, I started researching what should be our next steps.

My family and a few close friends had gathered to celebrate the birthday of a dear cousin (who was more like a brother) who had passed a year earlier. As we tend to do, we spent time catching up with each person, and I had a chance to reconnect with one of his best friends. I was able to share with him that I was starting a nonprofit organization. My sister, who is part of the team, was there as I explained to this friend the mission and purpose for the organization. "Wow! That is huge! I'd love to support you in that" was his immediate response. I appreciated his emphatic response, although I had no idea what "support" entirely meant.

Weeks later, I received a phone call from him stating that he had a building for our program. As it turns out, he is a real estate developer who owns a lot of property! That building was too big for us, perhaps mentally, more than anything else. It was an eighteen-unit apartment building in an area outside of the city. Although the team and I ultimately decided that it was not a good fit for us, the friend did not give up. He was persistent in wanting to help us. As I sat and waited, he said to me, "Go and develop your program. I've got you for your property."

And he did. A couple of months later, he found and offered us a smaller property in a good location for our program. The process went quickly, from receiving a phone call at work to view the property, to receiving the building as a gift before that workday ended.

Me: "Gift?"

Friend: "Gift! I told you I wanted to help you, and I want to gift Sistah's House with a building. I want nothing from you other than for you to be successful. Go, create your program."

So, we did. We began creating the program, working through the ins and outs of how we would help the young women we encountered. As the program moved from vision to feasibility, we soon discovered that we needed money, a lot of money to provide the services that were required. We held a few fundraisers, which brought in some money. But as I looked at what we needed compared with what we had; I began to get scared again. I saw that this was a more significant task than I had ever, ever imagined. But God is a big God, and that is what I had to come to grips with. I had heard it for so many years, and now I had to settle within myself that my God is as big as I accept him to be.

Soon, the next opportunity presented itself when a young lady walked through our church doors one summer afternoon. She had pearly white teeth and beautiful skin. And she was homeless. Her entire possessions were in the two suitcases she carried as she entered our building: one containing her clothes, and the other, a blow-up bed. There was nothing about her that appeared homeless. She was young, maybe twenty-three years old, and looked as if she had just stepped out of her house headed to work. I never knew the full story of why she was homeless, but she had nowhere to call home.

I spent the entire day trying to find her somewhere to safely lay her head. I realized that there was no place for her. First, I took her to the Pacific Garden Mission, a well-known shelter in Chicago. Their intake person kindly but honestly told us that the Mission was not the place for the young lady. "She's pretty, she doesn't look like she belongs here, and they will try to eat her alive tonight," she said.

As we moved on to the next shelter, and the next, I eventually realized that there was no place for someone like her. And I longed for a place of my own to shelter her.

We finally landed at Safe Haven, a shelter that provides a safe place for teens and young adults to get off the streets for the night. It is not a place to call home, but it is a safe place to sleep, shower, and have a hot meal. It was her best option.

I took her there, and I promised her that if she stayed true to her mission, that she would look back on this day, and she would be ok. As best I could, I encouraged her not to give up, and that I would not give up on her either.

With hope and a plan, she moved into the place where she could lay her head safely at night and not worry about someone taking advantage of her. About (one time) every one or two weeks, I would go to see her, bringing whatever she needed from her suitcase of clothes that I stored until she was on her own again in three months. Eventually, she moved into Bedford Homes, a shelter facility that houses young women and men while helping them become self-sufficient. She stayed there for about a year, and I stayed in touch with her, offering the support and resources I could until she landed on her feet. She now has a good job, lives in a studio apartment, and is doing well.

This experience showed me that this was something that I was supposed to do. I continued to build our program on paper and make connections with various organizations. The mission of Sistah's House is to open the doors of service to receive young women like the one who walked through my door at work on that faithful summer day.

The mission for Sistah's House is to provide a safe, loving, nurturing environment that allows young women to become who they were created to be. The program serves women ages 18-24 who find themselves homeless and directionless. Through workshops, group discussions, and access to external services, Sistah's House offers a lifeline to those who are serious. We provide a unique, a la carte, and holistic approach to meeting young women exactly where they are, allowing them to take their individualized journey to self-sufficiency and independence.

By opening their minds and hearts and realizing they were created for a divine purpose, the young women who come to us become ready to tap into their divine purpose. Sistah's House not only provides a safe space for personal development, but we work with each woman, helping them overcome the obstacles that interrupted their lives. Each woman's program plan looks different because each woman has a different need and is at a different level in life. For those who are willing to follow the program's guidelines, Sistah's House is a place where they can be comfortable, a safe place where they can grow and prosper. It is not a kickback space, nor a place where their family and friends can visit. But it is a place that allows them to grow.

Sistah's House does not charge our program participants but does ask them to help maintain the property, so it is clean, comfortable, and safe for all. We are seeking funding partners who want to contribute to this vital work of helping young women. With your help, we can open our doors quickly, and the young women can receive the support they so readily deserve.

I am so excited to be able to help young women. I am so excited for what God has in store for my team and me because we all have a passion for serving God's people.

—Crystal Crockett

AFTERWORD
A COLLABORATIVE WORK

Crystal J. Crockett – Chicago, Illinois
Calvin W. Denson – Decatur, Georgia
Harry Dock – Richton Park, Illinois
Dr. Janice Hooker Fortman – Calumet City, Illinois
Beverly Hammond – Houston, Texas/Metro
Focus James – Philadelphia, Pennsylvania
Wanisha Johnson – Chicago, Illinois
Michael Bart Mathews – Flossmoor, Illinois
Michael Perkins – Flossmoor, Illinois
Constance B. Thompson – Alpharetta, Georgia
Dr. Joseph Webb III – Miami, Florida

We decided to band together and write this book during the height of the COVID-19 pandemic that is sweeping our global communities. As our world will be forever changed, we must change along with the change! While we all are concerned about the health of ourselves, our family, neighbors, and friends, we are also concerned about how we can offer products and services to others who are also experiencing the coronavirus pandemic. Because of your selflessness during this crisis, no words are appropriate. Thank you, thank you, thank you for stepping up with your chapter contributions.

We could not have achieved this collaborative effort without everyone saying YES! No one said maybe, no one said not now, and most importantly, no one said I CAN'T! We understood that our many years of experience had prepared us for this transitional moment in time. We accepted this possible mission because we wanted to become a beacon of illumining light—an empowering source of energy. And a higher level of frequency by delivering purpose-driven, guided steps of self-awareness for those souls who are seeking personal and business achievement.

We wrote our chapters as if we were modern-day farmers planting seeds of experience, knowledge, and wisdom in the fields of our chapters. Each coauthor's chapter represents a different farmer, with a different area or message. The information in each chapter represents a different seed. Our collaborative efforts represent a vast amount of grains of wisdom. Each grain grew from deep down within our minds, thoughts, and life experiences. Acting as mental farmers, we spent hours, upon hours tilling out the negative weeds within our thoughts. We spent even more hours, upon hours planting, tilling, cultivating, and transforming our messages into seeds of plenty, positivity, purpose, passion, desire, faith, and action. The results from our harvest are highlighted in the pages of our contributions.

Our collective purpose was, and is, to share our message of hope, faith, desire, definiteness of purpose, and achievement within the hearts, minds, bodies, and souls of our readers. We chose to accept a difficult mission! A possible mission of helping our readers to change the way they look at things, so the things they look at would change! We gathered in unison, as a group of liked-minded Tribal Thought Leaders. We all were willing, ready, and able to deliver our transformational messages of realization and self-actualization within our chapters. We excepted a possible mission of transforming those eager souls who are seeking to find their WHY and live their PURPOSE driven life.

We tapped into our feelings from our internal guiding systems. We discovered our unique talents and gifts from the universe. We understood how we could reverse engineer the old school definition of F.E.A.R meaning: False Evidence Appearing Real. Instead, we transformed F.E.A.R. into meaning: Feeling Excited And Ready! We offer a glimmer of faith, that if acted upon, would surely change the thoughts and minds of the wandering generality while shaping that same mind into becoming a meaningful specific in life.

Your job is to take action NOW! Become as busy as a beaver, getting started by getting your financial house in order. Work diligently like the ant until your action plan for success is clearly defined. Become tenacious like the mighty White Shark and the Lion - the King of the jungle, allowing nothing or no one to defeat you. Become your worker bee until you claim Queen Bee status for achievement on your road to obtaining "that special something" that you desire! Finally, with your legacy secure, serve others by giving a hand up rather than a handout! Allow others also to taste the sweet honey (achievement and success) made from your definiteness of purpose.

—Michael Bart Mathews

ACKNOWLEDGEMENTS

Dr. James Dentley III

I want to thank my friend and Coach, Dr. James Dentley III, author of *The 5 Frequencies of High Performance,* for taking time out of your busy schedule to write the Foreword. I remember when we first met during one of your Sunday Inspired2Speak events held at NBC University – Networking, Business, and Coaching. That following Wednesday, you allowed me to speak on your stage in front of a full house of entrepreneurs, speakers, coaches, and business owners. The next week, Robbie and I spoke on your stage. We became certified speakers with you and Les Brown while attending your Inspired2Speak speakers camp.

You opened so many doors that allowed us (Mike and Robbie) to meet and learn from some of the best of the best, and for that, I am forever grateful. I express my humbleness and attitude of gratitude for your service-driven leadership, coaching, and, more importantly, our friendship.

Natalie M. Bonomo

I want to express my heartfelt gratitude to another friend, Natalie M. Bonomo, for her many hours of behind-the-scenes leadership that enabled this book collaboration project to flow. Your many years of being a high achieving corporate professional is one of your many assets. From start to finish, Natalie used her many years of literary talent and experience to shine the illuminating light on each author's chapter submission in a professional manner. Natalie clearly understood the level of her commitment needed for accomplishment.

After offering Natalie the opportunity to become a published author, she submitted her chapter in my book, *Finding Your Moment of Clarity: Discover Your Power Within.* After that achievement, I encouraged her to write her book. Natalie wrote and published her book, *Your Greatest Potential! Master Your Thinking.*

Having worked with Natalie in the past, I knew she could deliver the necessary final editing leadership that was required. Her style is to complement and enhance; however, never diminish, or take away from the creative content of each author's chapter submission. Thank you, Natalie, for joining forces with me and the list of exceptional authors who contributed to the completion of this book.

Robbie S. Mathews

Your support in the many different creative projects that I/ we embark on has proven to be invaluable. Trust, faith, due diligence, action planning, and teamwork have allowed our dream to work. Masterminding together along our journey has been one of several master keys to achievement. There is no I in the word team, and we make a great team. Love you!

—Michael Bart Mathews

ABOUT THE AUTHORS

In Order Of Appearance

Michael Bart Mathews

Co-Founder – The Mathews Entrepreneur Group, Inc

Photo by JC Penny

M ichael "Bart" Mathews, along with his wife Robbie, are the co-founders of The Mathews Entrepreneur Group – USA/Global. Michael is a successful Entrepreneur, Real Estate Investor, International Speaker, Author, and Manuscript Development Coach. He coaches his clients on "How to Get Your Book Out of Your Head So It Can Be Read." His first book, *Financially Speaking*, was published in 2008; the second edition published in 2016. Monetizing his thirteen years of experience in the literary industry, Michael's third book, *Finding Your Moment of Clarity* (Michael coached nine authors from five different countries), was published in 2019. Michael is a Certified Life Coach and Certified Speaker with Inspired2Speak founder and business strategist, Dr. James Dentley, and master motivator, Les Brown.

Michael had the pleasure of interviewing Al Pacino, "The Godfather," in front of over 2,000 attendees from several different countries. After internationally speaking together in South Africa, Robbie had the pleasure of interviewing Nelson

Mandela's grandson, Ndaba Mandela. The couple has been in the company of highly successful people such as John Travolta/ Actor, 50 Cent-Rapper/Actor, Mark Walberg /Actor, Steve Wozniak/Apple, Wesley Snipes/Actor, Randi Zuckerberg/former Facebook, Frank Shankwitz/Make-A-Wish Foundation, Kofi Annan/Former Secretary-General and joint Nobel Peace Prize winner with the United Nations, Steve Forbes/Forbes Magazine, Mirela Sula/Global Woman/Man Magazine and Club Founder, Veronica "Momma" Chew Tan/Success Resources, JT Foxx, Les Brown, Jeff Hoffman/Priceline, Drs. James and Kara Dentley/ Inspired2Speak Business Accelerator, Bill Walsh/Power Team International, Mark Victor Hansen, and Jack Canfield/Authors, among others.

On July 15, 2017, Michael and Robbie, shared the stage with Suzanne Le' Mignot-CBS Channel 2 News Journalist, D. Channsin Berry-Film Producer, Cynda Williams-Actress (Spike Lee), Tony Grant-Singer/Actor (Tyler Perry) and event organizer Quinton de' Alexander at the "We Dream In Color Humanitarian Celebration," in Chicago. Michael received the 2017 Businessman of the Year Award, named after John H. Johnson, founder of Ebony and Jet Magazine.

Michael was a member of the Hirsch High 1973 Boys Chicago City and Illinois High School Association Class AA State Basketball Championship Teams. Both teams were inducted into the Illinois High School Association (IHSA) Hall of Fame in 1993 and the Chicago Public League Basketball Coaches Association (CPLBCA) Hall of Fame in 2013. Michael was inducted into the Chicago Hirsch High School Alumni Hall of Fame Class of 2016. Michael did his undergraduate studies at Lincoln University in Jefferson City, Missouri, and the UW-Parkside in Kenosha, Wisconsin, where he played basketball at both universities. Michael spent thirty years in transportation. He held various management positions in the private sector and operator/line instructor positions in the public sector before retiring from the Chicago Transit Authority in 2012. He regularly donated to HBCU's scholarship funds using payroll deductions.

FOR YOUR FREE 30-MINUTE MANUSCRIPT DEVELOPMENT CONSULTATION, email your request to wecreatebooks@gmail.com. TO RECEIVE YOUR FREE GIFT, visit Michael at:

https://www.tmeginc.com/specialgift
https://www.linkedin.com/in/michaelbartmathews
https://www.facebook.com/michaelbartmathews
https://Instagram.com/michaelbartmathews
https://Twitter.com/mikemath73
Direct: 708-997-3508
WhatsApp: +1-708-997-3508 (International)
Email: wecreatebooks@gmail.com

Dr. Janice Hooker Fortman

Photo by Scott R. Gane

Janice Hooker Fortman, Ed.D, DTM, is an Effective Communication Strategist, motivational speaker, and author. Her mission is to improve the personal and professional lives of people by giving them peace and power by improving their communication skills. Jan believes that communication is the foundation for all relationships; therefore, people's opinions of you are formed by the way you communicate both verbally and nonverbally.

She is a member of the Chicago Writers Association, Women's Speakers Association, and was recognized by the International Association of Women as the 2013/2014 Professional Woman of the Year for leadership in public speaking. Age Options, an agency that provides self-management skills for older adults with ongoing health conditions, honored her service as an outstanding volunteer from 2014 to 2019.

As the author of the award-winning book, *The Secrets to How NOT to Throw Mama from the Train*, she focuses on the relationship between adult daughters and their aging mothers and the communication patterns that cause difficulties in this relationship. Her related workshops, coaching, and presentations offer insight, advice, and solutions on resolving conflicts in this complicated and dynamic relationship.

Her book, *The Little Book of BIG Behavior Interventions,* presents the common misbehaviors of Pre-K and elementary school children and the nonverbal communication that forecasts misbehavior. Her keen insight on why young children misbehave in their classrooms is popular with teachers who are faced with the challenging misbehaviors of their students. She also presents "Independent Thinking Skills," a motivational workshop for adults and children who need assistance in setting life and professional goals. Jan is happily married to her husband, Keith, who is a two-time cancer survivor. They both enjoy traveling and supporting various nonprofit organizations.

Contact Dr. Jan for your initial consultation concerning your core values that align with her content. Follow her on social media. Take time out and get to know more about her empowering programs!

1-877-66-SPEAK
www.drjanicespeaks.com
jan4now125@gmail.com and https://www.youtube/channel/
UC-FrDSfOb4j-dXDst5297aQ/about
https://www.linkedin.com/drjanicehookerfortman/
https://www.twitter.com/drJTLH

Dr. Joseph Webb III, CKA, CRFA, CLTC, DD

Profit Planners Management Group LLC

Photo by Carnival Cruise Lines

My name is Joseph Webb III, CRFA, CLTC, DD. I am a Registered Investment Financial Advisor, and the Profit Planners Management Group Registered Principal.

My professional career focuses on providing investment services, asset protection, tax strategies, specialized insurances, and survivor assistance to individuals. I pride myself on demonstrating a serious commitment to my clients and the community. I help my clients reach the next level of financial success through seminars, financial counseling, debt relief, and comprehensive financial planning. I currently hold a life, health, and annuity license, along with the series 6, 7, 24, 26, 63, and 65 security licenses.

I hold the position of Director of Life and Family Empowerment at New Jerusalem PBC. I have been an active member of the following organizations: the Business Network International (Vision Chapter), the Christian Chamber of Greater Miami

(Board Member), the Military Affairs Committee of the South Dade Chamber of Commerce (Board Member), the Greater Miami Fellowship of Christian Athletes (Advisory Board Member), and the Goulds Coalition of Ministers and Lay People, Homestead Professional Business Group (Former Board Member). I serve as a mentor for the "5000 Role Models of Excellence Project," and I am the President of the Society of Certified Retirement Financial Advisors (CRFA).

I received my financial education through Kaplan Financial University. I received a bachelor's degree in nonprofit management and a master's degree in Christian education from St. Thomas Christian University (STCU). I was awarded by STCU an Honorary Doctorate for my work in God's financial vineyard over the past 15 years. Lastly, I served our country in the Air Force Reserves for more than thirty years.

I share in the mission of the South Dade Chamber of Commerce, as evident through my service. I aspire to "strengthen the economy of South Miami-Dade and enhance the quality of life for our residents and visitors. Using programs of voluntary action to preserve and protect the American system of a free competitive enterprise system. To advance the economic, civic education, cultural and social well-being of the South Dade community." I currently hold the position as Chairman of the South Dade Chamber of Commerce.

With my background in comprehensive financial planning and my vast experience in serving on numerous boards, I am dedicated to strengthening our local community.

JOSEPH WEBB III, CKA, CRFA, CLTC, DD
PROFIT PLANNERS MANAGEMENT GROUP, LLC
FINANCIAL ADVISOR/PLANNER
(305) 905-1055
www.profitplannersmg.com
joewebb@profitplannersmg.com

MICHAEL PERKINS

Photo by Braxton McCarroll

M ichael Perkins is a business coach, financial consultant, and dedicated advocate for entrepreneurs. He is a published author and speaker. He provides strategic solutions for entrepreneurs and real estate investors who are starting businesses or want to grow their current business more quickly. His primary focus is on assisting entrepreneurs with developing their referral network. He also helps investors with accessing capital to fund their businesses. He is committed to assisting them with building credit, generating revenue, accumulating assets, and building wealth.

Michael intends to use his platform as the founder of Tribal Wealth United to assist 600 other socially conscious entrepreneurs with starting their businesses to help strengthen families and build sustainable communities. Michael is a business collaboration expert who works with brand ambassadors and influencers to cultivate mutually beneficial relationships. The result is that all parties magnify their influence, impact, and income by practicing collaborative economics.

In his chapter, "It Takes a Tribe to Raise a Village," Michael explores "Four Keys to Promoting a Membership Site to Build an

Online Business." Entrepreneurs who are serious about building an online business that generates recurring income should implement these concepts without delay. These key concepts will position members to follow a successful path to achieve financial freedom.

Michael has been married to his wife Elaine since 2000 and currently resides in Flossmoor, Illinois. He is a graduate of the Loyola University of Chicago and a senior associate in Financial Services.

Michael Perkins
Founder, Tribal Wealth United
Direct: 773-297-1594
Website: www.tribalwealthunited.com

CALVIN W. DENSON, SR.

Denson Financial Services, Owner

Photo by Artanza Denson

C alvin provides accounting, financial classes, consulting, and income tax services to churches, individuals, nonprofit organizations, and small businesses.

He is a licensed independent insurance agent in life, health, property, and casualty insurance. An ordained minister, Calvin volunteers at the House of Hope Atlanta as the Prison Ministry Coordinator. Calvin is the team leader for ministers while serving on the Prayer, Social Justice, and Men's Ministry. He teaches financial education classes at the Federal Half-Way House (Dismas, Inc.) and the County Jail. He is a financial professional with experience in accounting, financial planning, insurance, and tax preparation. Calvin previously worked in corporate financial positions for Rockwell, Scientific-Atlanta, Morganite North America (Dulmison), Tyco Electronics, RTI International, and various major insurance companies.

Calvin is a product of the Muskegon, Michigan public school system, attending from elementary through high school.

After graduation, he attended Muskegon Community College, receiving his Associate of Arts degree while playing varsity basketball. He continued his education at the University of Wisconsin-Parkside in Kenosha, Wisconsin, receiving his Bachelor of Science degree in Business Management/Accounting. He also played varsity basketball in his senior year. That team advanced to the Elite Eight of the NAIA Playoff Basketball Tournament. In 2014, the team was inducted into the school's Sports Hall of Fame.

He attended the New Life Community of Ministry and Bible Institute in Raleigh, North Carolina, receiving his Associate, Bachelor, and Master of Religion.

Calvin resides in the Greater Atlanta, Georgia area with his wife, where he can be close to his children and grandchildren. He is available for speaking engagements, seminars, and personal consultation in financial, insurance, and ministry. He likes to relate ministry to finance and enjoys helping others improve financially and spiritually.

Calvin W. Denson, Sr.
Denson Financial Services
919-889-0463
densoncalvin@yahoo.com
Facebook
LinkedIn

HARRY DOCK

Photo by Arnold Taylor

H arry Dock is an experienced businessman having been
in corporate America for the past fifty years. Dock's
education was in the foodservice industry, hospitality, and hotel
management. Over thirty years, Dock was able to accomplish
many personal, business, and service-driven goals, which
propelled him to success. He has been the recipient of many
performance awards throughout his illustrious career. Being an
early pioneer in the service industry, Dock became a co-owner
of a food and beverage operation at a country club located in
Northeast Ohio. He flourished at the corporate management
level.

Dock was born and raised in Leeds, Alabama. The entire Dock
family were hard workers. Because of his work ethic, Harry
excelled, by being anchored within the family structure and the
surrounding community.

The Dock family decided to leave the South and crossed over
the Mason-Dixon Line while coming north. Moving north was
a challenge for his family; however, his mother was determined
to make it happen. She understood that there were bigger and
better opportunities up north, versus being down south!

The family motto was, "If we stick together, we can make it." Harry realized that education was the key, and this would take him places that he would never imagine possible had his family not left the South. Harry received a scholarship that allowed him to attend junior college. This act became a uniquely valuable learning experience that ultimately became the launching pad toward corporate success.

After thirty years in the service and hospitality industry, it was time to make a career change. Harry Dock stepped out on faith and made a bold decision. In the year 2000, Harry became a loan officer, and within two years, he became an office manager. After the crash of the housing market, Harry started his mortgage consulting firm. He assisted homeowners who had been victimized by the mortgage crisis in 2009. Harry Dock is currently semi-retired. He is helping his clients with the ins and outs of real estate.

Harry Dock resides in Richton Park, Illinois, while being married to his lovely wife for two years. They have four children.

Harry Dock
DockHarry1@yahoo.com

Focus James

Certified Life Coach/Public Speaker/Trainer/Biz Coach

Photo by Albert Willis

Since her playground days in elementary school, Focus has been speaking up for the underdog. Throughout the years, her passion for the growth and development of children and young adults compelled her to earn a degree in early childhood education. With her passion, education, and experience, Focus can speak to the little girl or boy that is inside each of us. She received her degree in communications, theater, broadcast, and journalism. This led Focus to become a master of communication and enhanced her ability to hear beyond spoken words, breathing life into untold stories.

Her latest accomplishments include becoming certified as a transformational life coach, teacher, trainer, and speaker from the world-renowned John C. Maxwell team. The John C. Maxwell organization is the #1 producer of leaders and coaches worldwide. She received a speaker's certificate awarded by Inspire2speak, a program organized by James Dentley and the master motivator and storyteller, Les Brown. Focus is the author of *What is The Focus of Love?* A book stocked full of breakthroughs and aha moments of transformational content.

With her extensive training in coaching and leadership, her dynamic and engaging speaking abilities, and her compassion, and drive, Focus will help you propel your life forward to your desired destination. With Focus as your coach, teacher, and trainer, you will be able to have the life you love and have the ability to create the skills needed to live on your highest frequency and build core beliefs and habits that serve your highest being. With her dynamic curriculum, your organization will be astonished at its ability to achieve what you have been longing to do! Let the journey begin!

Testimonial

From Focus's coaching, I realized I was focused on 'being right' in my relationships, and that was not healthy for either of us. Focus helped me to understand how layered relationships are and that there are just as many layers to healing from relationships. I am on a journey of peeling back those layers gently and graciously overtime to heal strategically in order to have the least amount of scarring, taking responsibility for my part, and crystalizing what I actually do want as I gain my self-worth. Thank you, Focus, for who you are!
—Kiara T., Philadelphia

I take this time to say a big thank you, Focus, for your dedication for helping me realize my greatness. After just three sessions you were able to help me see that I had great ideas, and I needed to get them out or, better said, get out of my head. After three sessions, I feel like I have already gotten my money's worth. I am so excited to see what it will be like at the end of all my sessions. Thank you.
—Michale A., Nova Scotia, by way of Grenada

Ms. Focus James
Company Name/Title: The Focus Of Love LLC/CEO
Contact: 267-978-1247
Website: www.focusjames.com
Email: focus@focusjames.com

Social Media:
https://www.facebook.com/focus.james.3
https://www.facebook.com/WhatisTheFocusOfLove/
https://www.instagram.com/thefocusoflove/
https://www.linkedin.com/in/focus-james/

CONSTANCE B. THOMPSON

Photo by Constance B. Thompson

I am Constance B. Thompson. I was born and raised on the southside of Chicago in the Englewood Community. My parents, Mose and Vanilla (Mitchell) Bennett, had ten children, and I am the youngest! The good thing about being the youngest child is that I was able to watch my siblings as I grew up and see if I wanted to be like any of them. The answer was no!

I believed I was brainwashed by watching two soap operas: All My Children and Dynasty. I thought Erica Kane (Susan Lucie), an actor on All My Children, and Dominique Deveraux (Diahann Carroll), an actor on Dynasty, had it all together. They were strong, powerful, beautiful women who dressed well, and lived in beautiful homes in charming neighborhoods. I liked everything about them. Well, not everything, but most things. I tried to mimic them.

I was in high school, and probably about sixteen years old when I enrolled in modeling school. I thought I was on my way to being amongst my idols, Erica and Dominique. This was when I started to live out my true love for beautification. In the 80s, there were no makeup artists or glam squads I could call upon. I was my own glam squad. I had to buy and bring my clothes to the set and do my makeup. By doing so, I learned very quickly how to *beat* my face. Putting outfits together was no problem for me because my parents were *fly* dressers.

The word fly means very well-dressed. That was the word people used in the 80s. If someone thought you were dressed well, they would either say, "Girl, you know you are looking fly, or you dressed to the nines." Anyway, my parents were both great dressers. When it came time for me to pick out outfits for the stage, it was a breeze.

I kept myself busy every summer during my school years. After graduation, I decided that I was going to lay back and chill with my sisters only to learn that they did not have the same desire. They thought I was *square* or lame. I was left alone. My girlfriend next door, Valerie, would come over to get me out of the house. We sat on the front porch, talked, and laughed. We listened to music and occasionally walked around the block. One day, I asked, "Why are we walking around the block for no reason?" She said, "Girl, we are walking so we can look for boys." Rolling my eyes, thinking, "Is this what she got me out the house for?" At that time, boys were not on my radar; besides, I already had a boyfriend. I was trying to figure out how I could get a lifelike Erica Kane and Dominique Deveraux.

As the years went by, our neighborhood deteriorated. The neighborhood kids I went to school with were turning into alcoholics, drug addicts, and gang bangers. All I wanted was to get out of the neighborhood and have a better life. I wanted to be in a beautiful community like ours used to be when we first moved there, and I just did not know how to do it.

One day, my girlfriend Valerie and I were sitting on the porch, and she said, "Robin across the street just got back from the Air Force." I said, "Air Force?" She said, "Yes!" Then I said, "That's it!" She said, "What's it?" I said, "That's how I'm going to get out this neighborhood." She said, "By going to the Air Force?" I said, "No! By going into the military." And this is how my life journey, my personal development, really began.

Beverly Hammond

Photo by Benjamin Hammond

When Beverly Hammond, the oldest of four children, was a young girl, her paternal grandmother would observe Beverly's interactions with her siblings. The grandmother would often remark that Beverly would become a schoolteacher. Beverly did not see that as a career choice for her because she had an insatiable desire to travel and see the world.

Beverly chose a twenty-year military career in the U.S. Air Force as a computer technologist, which afforded her the chance to travel the world. But coincidentally, she fulfilled her dreams to travel and her grandmother's prediction of becoming a teacher. Her expertise was leveraged to train thousands of military and government employees on computer systems.

After military retirement, Beverly continued professionally as a database consultant. Over the next fifteen years, she added another 5,000 trained corporate employees to her resume. During this same period, Beverly began reinventing herself. Looking for a new life path, she and her husband, Benjamin, participated in various activities.

Despite the personal successes, Beverly gained firsthand knowledge of the wealth gap between Black families and other ethnic groups. By 2016, her awareness of these disparities had elevated to a conviction for making a difference.

After more than thirty-five years of teaching technology, she launched Black Wealth Consortium (BWC) in December of 2017 to continue teaching. BWC is a platform that provides training and mentorship of wealth-building strategies to Black families. With members in over fourteen states, BWC is positioning its members to become change agents within Black communities across the United States and eventually around the world.

It seems that Beverly became a technologist, but she was born a teacher. It looks like Grandma knew what she was talking about!

Bev Hammond
Founder, Black Wealth Consortium
Direct: 832-703-4574
Fax: 866-832-1341

Wanisha "Logic" Johnson

Photo by Wanisha Johnson

I have always been a talker and a listener. Even as a child, I always had something of substance to say. Or some sound advice to give and an impactive way of giving it. Words are commanding, connecting, and they do have power.

I am Wanisha Johnson, and I was born and raised on the south side of Chicago. My parents met while employed at the U.S. Post Office. They fell in love, married, and I came thereafter. Growing up in Chicago, you must develop tough skin. Things happen, life happens, and most of us were not taught the skill sets needed to deal with adversity. We must prepare them with each new experience. I have always been a "take care of the inside of you" type of person. That is what matters most. My main message is that every day we should make a conscious effort to be better. And it is never too late to accomplish anything.

Chicago is a beautiful city filled with diversity. That is one of my favorite thoughts of the city. I have visited many cities, and home will always be there, on the south side. I went to private schools for middle school and high school. I then went on to get my CDL to be an over-the-road driver. After two years, I returned home to become a real estate professional. I enjoy traveling and selling homes, but I have been a writer all my life.

I battled with stage fright and not wanting to be in the spotlight. I never wanted to be at the mercy of applause or ridicule. But there comes a time when you reclaim and dismiss as needed.

As I grew up, I became more aware of the world and the situations around me. My mission is to reach, deep down, to where most people do not want to get their hands dirty. Some of my spoken word, purposely seeks out the people in the back, the discouraged, the abandoned, the dismissed. They feel the things that most do not speak about. I believe people can be pulled out of the trenches with words. Not everyone is on edge, but a lot of people are. I have a strong sense of compassion, and that is what I put into words.

My next mission is to spread my message and publish the book of spoken word that I have been creating. It is time to grow in that area as well. Everything is about moving forward. There are times you may have to stand still—but—you are still standing. And sometimes that is enough. Just do not go backward. If you do not dare to run toward your dreams and goals, taking baby steps will get you there.

Wanisha Johnson – LogicNMotion

CRYSTAL J. CROCKETT

Sistah's House of New Beginnings

Photo by Mandel Golden

Crystal J. Crockett has a deep passion and a long history of working with and serving youth, especially young women. Her action-based energy for serving the community at a higher level is what led Crystal to create, and officially launch, Sistah's House of New Beginnings. Along with several other co-founding members, Crystal's unwavering dedication is to serve, uplift, empower, and transform the lives of youth and young women is now her burning desire for achievement!

Crystal is not motivated by wealth, not by fortune, and certainly not by fame. Crystal, along with Sistah's House of New Beginnings, has a spiritual guiding light with a mission to serve one young woman at a time. Crystal decided to pursue higher education and now capitalizes on her learning experiences.

Crystal holds a master's degree in specialized education from Quincy University and a bachelor's degree in healthcare and business management from DeVry University. She has worked with and served youth for well over twenty years. She is still incredibly passionate about offering a hand up, not a handout, using her various programs for success in each young woman's life journey.

Her professional experience, training, and skillsets are utilized through her personalized mentoring programs, nurturing sessions, and mature guidance intervention initiatives. These programs are focused on preparing young women for living life after Sistah's House. Crystal administers the personalized mentoring program for each young woman and oversees the day-to-day operations of the transitional home.

Crystal is a native of the south side of Chicago. While growing up in a two-parent home, Crystal credits her mother with providing intentional social direction while exposing her family to a broad array of real-life cultural experiences. This early-in-life foundation laid the groundwork for Crystal's life-long pursuit of service while helping her understand how important education and excellent life skills were to advancing personal development and a world of opportunities for others.

Crystal is a mother to two sons, and a mother figure to many young women and men throughout Chicago. Crystal attended Burnside Elementary and Percy L. Julian Public schools in Chicago, and she is a lifetime member of Christ Universal Temple.

Crystal Crockett
Direct: 708.925.8898
Email: sistahshouse@gmail.com
Website: https://sistahshouse.org

With sincere gratitude for every contributor within the pages of this book, we offer you our final mission.

YOUR CALL TO ACTION

"There is never time in the future in which we will work out our salvation. The challenge is in the moment; the time is always now." – James Baldwin

"I have discovered in life that there are ways of getting where you want to go, if you really want to go." – Langston Hughes

We invite you to connect with the author that best resonates with you, your mission, and your core values. Decide who can best walk with you along your journey of personal development, business development, financial achievement, real estate, insurance, communication skills, love & relationships, overcoming real life challenges and your willingness to serve others at a higher level. Reread each author's chapter and bio carefully. Each chapter is only a small snapshot of the help, training, and assistance that each author can offer.

You can communicate directly with the author of your choice. No middleman, no buffering! Schedule your private discovery session directly with one or all of us. Doing so will allow you the opportunity to get to know the author of your choice on a more personal, private, and confidential level.

If you do not know where you are going, how will you know when you get there? Imagine achieving that special something that you desire? Think about which author can help you achieve your visions, goals, and dreams. Now think about the many people who are depending on you to succeed, for them to succeed.

You will find our contact information at the end of the About the Author section. Your next coach is just a phone call or email away!

Let us help you to achieve "that special something" that you desire most in life.

Printed in the United States
By Bookmasters